Incredibly Easy
Silly Snacks

Publications International, Ltd.
Favorite Brand Name Recipes at www.fbnr.com

Front cover photography and photography on pages 11, 23, 29, 35, 55, 61, 75, 79, 115, 117,
135 and 145 by Tony Glaser Photography.

Photography on pages 45, 49, 53, 57, 85 and 141 by Proffitt Photography, Chicago.

Recipes on pages 10, 16, 22, 44, 48 top, 52 top, 56, 78, 100, 104, 112, 114, 134, 147
and 152 developed by Alison Reich.

Recipes on pages 28, 34, 47, 48 bottom, 52 bottom, 62, 74, 84, 90, 96, 110, 116, 140, 144
and 146 developed by Marcia Kay Stanley, M.S., R.D.

Pictured on the front cover: Chocolate Chip Cannoli Cones *(page 134).*

Pictured on the back cover: Spotted Butterfly Sandwich *(page 44).*

ISBN-13: 978-1-4127-2548-4
ISBN-10: 1-4127-2548-8

Library of Congress Control Number: 2006939552

Manufactured in China.

8 7 6 5 4 3 2 1

Microwave Cooking: Microwave ovens vary in wattage. Use the cooking times as
guidelines and check for doneness before adding more time.

Preparation/Cooking Times: Preparation times are based on the approximate amount
of time required to assemble the recipe before cooking, baking, chilling or serving.
These times include preparation steps such as measuring, chopping and mixing. The fact
that some preparations and cooking can be done simultaneously is taken into account.
Preparation of optional ingredients and serving suggestions is not included.

Contents

Light Bites   4

Lunchtime Treats   36

Party Time   68

Afternoon Nibbles   102

Sweet Snacks   126

Acknowledgments   155

Index   156

BLT Cukes
(p. 12)

Sweet Potato Spread
Sandwich (p. 10)

Breakfast Mice
(p. 18)

Peanut Butter-Apple
Wraps (p. 22)

Light Bites

Banana Caterpillars

2 medium bananas
¼ cup peanut butter
¼ cup flaked coconut
4 raisins
6 thin pretzel sticks

1. Peel and cut each banana into 10 slices. Assemble "caterpillar" by spreading slices with peanut butter and pressing pieces together.

2. Sprinkle half of coconut over each "caterpillar" and press lightly with fingertips to coat. Use additional peanut butter to adhere raisins on one end to form "eyes." Break pretzel sticks into small pieces and press between banana slices for "legs" and "antenna." Serve immediately.

Makes 2 servings

Tip: Kids can also be creative and add other types of sliced fruits (strawberries, apples, pears) to their caterpillars.

Watermelon Kebobs

18 (1-inch) cubes seedless watermelon
6 ounces (1-inch cubes) fat-free turkey breast
6 ounces (1-inch cubes) reduced-fat Cheddar cheese
6 (6-inch) bamboo skewers or plastic straws

Alternate cubes of watermelon between cubes of turkey and cheese threaded onto each skewer or straw, as shown in photo.

Makes 6 servings

Favorite recipe from **National Watermelon Promotion Board**

Funny Face Pizza Snacks

4 English muffins, split
½ cup pizza sauce or low-fat pasta sauce
¾ cup part-skim shredded mozzarella cheese
Vegetables and ham or pepperoni

Preheat oven to 350°F.

Lightly toast English muffins in toaster. Arrange on a baking sheet and spread each muffin with sauce, then top with cheese. Cut vegetables and meat into shapes as suggested below. Bake for 12 to 15 minutes or until cheese melts.

Makes 8 servings

Suggestions for faces: Eyes: olives, mushrooms or carrot strips. Nose: cherry tomato half, zucchini slice, mushroom, pepperoni or ham. Mouth: bell pepper slices or carrot strips. Hair: strips of ham, cauliflower or broccoli florets cut in small pieces.

Favorite recipe from **Wheat Foods Council**

Peachy Pops

Prep Time: 20 minutes • **Freeze Time:** 4 hours

1 package (16 ounces) frozen sliced peaches, softened not thawed
2 containers (8 ounces each) peach or vanilla yogurt
¼ cup honey
12 popsicle sticks or lollipop sticks
12 small paper cups
   Sugar sprinkles

1. Place peaches, yogurt and honey in food processor or blender container. Cover and process until mixture is fairly smooth, about 20 seconds, scraping down sides as needed.

2. Pour peach mixture into paper cups and place on baking sheet. Freeze peach mixture 1 hour or until mixture begins to harden. Push popsicle sticks into centers and freeze an additional 3 hours or until firm. Tear paper away from pops and roll in sugar sprinkles. Serve immediately or return to freezer until serving time. *Makes 12 (½ cup) servings*

Sweet Potato
Spread Sandwich

4 ounces sweet potato (about ½ sweet potato)
2 tablespoons water
2 tablespoons chopped walnuts
2 tablespoons dried cranberries
½ teaspoon ground cinnamon
2 teaspoons sugar substitute
4 slices light multi-grain bread, toasted
4 tablespoons fat-free whipped topping

1. Peel and chop sweet potato and place in glass dish. Sprinkle with water. Microwave on HIGH 6 minutes. Let cool and mash with cooking liquid.

2. Combine walnuts, cranberries, cinnamon and sugar substitute in medium bowl. Stir in potato.

3. Divide sweet potato mixture between 2 slices toast, spread whipped topping over sweet potato mixture and cover with other slice of toast. Cut into halves. *Makes 4 servings*

BLT Cukes

3 slices crisp-cooked bacon, chopped
½ **cup finely chopped lettuce**
½ **cup finely chopped baby spinach**
¼ **cup diced tomato**
1½ **tablespoons fat-free mayonnaise**
   Pinch salt
¼ **teaspoon black pepper**
1 **large cucumber**
   Minced parsley or green onion (optional)

1. Combine bacon, lettuce, spinach, tomato and mayonnaise. Season with salt and pepper; set aside.

2. Peel cucumber. Trim off ends and slice in half lengthwise. Use spoon to scoop out seeds; discard seeds. Divide BLT mixture between cucumber halves, mounding in hollowed areas. Garnish with parsley, if desired. Cut into 2-inch pieces. *Makes 8 to 10 pieces*

Note: Make these snacks when cucumbers are large enough to easily hollow out with a spoon. You may make these up to 12 hours ahead of time and chill until ready to serve.

Orange You
Glad Dessert

Prep Time: 20 minutes • **Freeze Time:** 5 hours

4 naval oranges, halved
3 containers (8 ounces each) orange, lemon or vanilla yogurt
2 tablespoons frozen orange juice concentrate
1 teaspoon vanilla
Red food coloring (optional)
4 mint leaves (optional)

1. Carefully cut pulp from oranges with small knife and spoon. Place pulp in blender container. Reserve empty orange shells.

2. Process pulp, yogurt, orange juice concentrate, vanilla and food coloring, if desired, in blender until almost smooth, about 12 seconds.

3. Spoon orange mixture into 4 reserved orange halves, mounding mixture on top. Cover loosely with plastic wrap and freeze until firm, about 4 hours. Remove plastic wrap. Place remaining 4 orange halves on top of orange mixture. Place oranges in freezer-safe bowls; freeze at least 1 hour before serving. Garnish with mint leaves, if desired.

Makes 4 servings

Zucchini Circles

2 medium zucchini (about 12 ounces total)
1 egg
½ teaspoon salt
1 cup seasoned bread crumbs
2 tablespoons olive oil
1 tablespoon apricot jam
1 tablespoon honey
1 teaspoon water

1. Preheat oven to 350°F. Line baking sheet with foil and spray with nonstick cooking spray; set aside.

2. Cut zucchini crosswise into ¼-inch slices. Beat egg and salt in small bowl. Spread bread crumbs on plate. Dip zucchini slices into egg mixture and then into bread crumbs, coating both sides. Place on prepared baking sheet in single layer. Drizzle with oil and bake 25 minutes or until golden brown.

3. Meanwhile prepare dipping sauce. Place jam, honey and water in small microwavable dish. Microwave on HIGH 20 seconds or until warm; stir. Dip Zucchini Circles into sauce. *Makes 4 servings*

Baby Bran Muffins
with Citrus Spread

Bran Muffins

    1 cup whole bran cereal
    1 cup milk
    1 egg, beaten
    2 tablespoons butter, melted
    1 cup all-purpose flour
    ¼ cup packed brown sugar
  2½ teaspoons baking powder
    ½ teaspoon baking soda
    ¼ teaspoon salt
    ¼ teaspoon ground cinnamon
    ¼ cup currants

Citrus Spread

    1 package (8 ounces) cream cheese, softened
    3 tablespoons orange juice
    1 teaspoon granulated sugar

1. Preheat oven to 375°F. Spray 24 miniature (1¾-inch) muffin pan cups with nonstick cooking spray. Set aside.

2. Combine cereal, milk, egg and butter in large bowl. Set aside 10 minutes or until cereal is moistened. Combine flour, brown sugar, baking powder, baking soda, salt and cinnamon in large bowl. Add to bran mixture, stirring just until blended. Fold in currants.

3. Spoon batter into prepared muffin cups filling three-fourths full. Bake 15 minutes or until firm when lightly pressed. Let muffins stand 1 minute; remove to wire racks to cool.

4. To prepare Citrus Spread, beat cream cheese, orange juice and granulated sugar in large bowl with electric mixer at high speed 1 minute or until cream cheese is light and fluffy. Split open muffins and spread lightly with Citrus Spread. *Makes 24 mini muffins*

Tip: Leftover muffins can be frozen in resealable plastic food storage bag. Reheat in preheated 325°F oven for 5 minutes.

Warm Peanut-Caramel Dip

¼ cup reduced-fat peanut butter
2 tablespoons fat-free caramel ice cream topping
2 tablespoons fat-free (skim) milk
1 large apple, thinly sliced
4 large pretzel rods, broken in half

1. Combine peanut butter, caramel topping and milk in small saucepan. Heat over low heat, stirring constantly, until mixture is melted and warm.

2. Serve dip with apple slices and pretzel rods.   *Makes 4 servings*

Microwave Directions: Combine all ingredients except apple slices and pretzel rods in small microwavable dish. Microwave on MEDIUM (50%) 1 minute; stir well. Microwave an additional minute or until mixture is melted and warm.

Happy Apple Salsa with Baked Cinnamon Pita Chips

2 teaspoons sugar
¼ teaspoon cinnamon
2 pita bread rounds, split
  Nonstick cooking spray
1 tablespoon jelly or jam
1 apple, diced
1 tablespoon finely diced celery
1 tablespoon finely diced carrot
1 tablespoon raisins
1 teaspoon lemon juice

1. Preheat oven to 350°F.

2. Combine sugar and cinnamon in small bowl. Set aside.

3. Cut pita rounds into wedges and place on a baking sheet. Spray lightly with cooking spray and sprinkle with cinnamon-sugar mixture. Bake 10 minutes or until lightly browned; set aside to cool.

4. Meanwhile, place jelly in medium microwavable bowl and heat in microwave on HIGH 10 seconds. Stir in apple, celery, carrot, raisins and lemon juice. Serve salsa with pita chips.   *Makes 3 servings*

Breakfast Mice

2 hard-cooked eggs, peeled and halved lengthwise
2 teaspoons low-fat mayonnaise
¼ teaspoon salt
2 radishes, thinly sliced and root ends reserved
8 raisins or currants
1 ounce Cheddar cheese, shredded or cubed
  Spinach or lettuce leaves (optional)

1. Gently scoop egg yolks into small bowl. Mash yolks, mayonnaise and salt until smooth. Spoon yolk mixture back into egg halves. Place 2 halves, cut side down, on each serving plate.

2. Cut two tiny slits near the narrow end of each egg half; position 2 radish slices on each half for ears. Use the root end of each radish to form tails. Push raisins into each egg half to form eyes. Place small pile of cheese in front of each mouse. Garnish with spinach leaves, if desired.

Makes 2 servings

Jiggly
Banana Split

Prep Time: 5 minutes

3 gelatin snack cups (3 ounces each), any flavors
1 banana
3 tablespoons whipped topping
   Colored sprinkles
1 maraschino cherry

1. Unmold snack cups by dipping partially in warm water for a few seconds. Slide gelatin from cups into center of serving dish.

2. Peel banana and cut in half lengthwise. Place banana slices on each side of gelatin.

3. Top with dollops of whipped topping, sprinkles and cherry.

Makes 1 serving

Chillin' Out
Watermelon Soda

Prep Time: 10 minutes

¾ cup frozen orange-pineapple-apple juice concentrate, thawed
6 cups cubed seeded watermelon
2 cups sparkling water or club soda
  Ice cubes
6 small watermelon wedges

1. Combine juice concentrate and watermelon in blender container or food processor. Cover and process until smooth. Divide water and ice cubes among 6 glasses. Pour watermelon mixture over water in glasses. Stir to combine.

2. Garnish each with watermelon wedge.   *Makes 6 (8-ounce) servings*

Peaches and Creamy Dip with
Waffle Wedges

4 ounces (½ 8-ounce package) reduced-fat cream cheese
⅓ cup no-sugar-added peach preserves
1 tablespoon fat-free (skim) milk
2 packets sugar substitute
½ teaspoon vanilla
4 low-fat toaster waffles
  Ground cinnamon

1. Place all ingredients except waffles and cinnamon in blender container and process until smooth. Set aside.

2. Toast waffles; cut each waffle into 6 wedges.

3. Place cream cheese mixture in small serving bowl; sprinkle with cinnamon. Serve with waffle wedges for dipping.

Makes 24 wedges and about ¾ cup dip

Peanut Butter-Apple Wraps

Prep Time: 5 minutes • **Chill Time:** 2 hours

¾ **cup creamy peanut butter**
4 **(7-inch) whole wheat or spinach tortillas**
¾ **cup finely chopped apple**
⅓ **cup shredded carrot**
⅓ **cup low-fat granola without raisins**
1 **tablespoon toasted wheat germ**

Spread peanut butter on one side of each tortilla. Sprinkle each tortilla evenly with apple, carrot, granola and wheat germ. Roll up tightly; cut in half. Serve immediately or refrigerate until ready to serve.

Makes 4 servings

Luscious Veggie Sandwich Spread

1 **package (8 ounces) reduced-fat cream cheese, softened**
1 **to 2 tablespoons reduced-fat (2%) milk**
4 **ounces lean honey or brown sugar ham, finely chopped**
½ **cup finely chopped red or yellow bell pepper**
2 **tablespoons minced chives or green onion**
2 **tablespoons sweet pickle relish**
Mini bagels or whole wheat crackers

1. Beat cream cheese and milk in small bowl with electric mixer at medium speed until smooth. Stir in ham, bell pepper, chives and pickle relish. Cover and refrigerate for up to 2 days.

2. Serve as a spread on mini bagels or whole wheat crackers.

Makes about 2 cups

Variation: Spread can also be used to stuff hollowed-out cherry tomatoes or celery sticks.

Watermelon Dippers

8 ounces sour cream
¼ cup sugar
1 teaspoon vanilla extract
   Watermelon sticks or small wedges

Combine the sour cream, sugar and vanilla in a small serving bowl; stir until well blended. Use as a dip for the watermelon.

Makes about 8 servings

Favorite recipe from **National Watermelon Promotion Board**

Banana Tot Pops

Prep Time: 20 minutes • **Freeze Time:** 2 hours

3 firm, medium DOLE® Bananas
6 large wooden sticks
½ cup raspberry or other flavored yogurt
1 jar (1¾ ounces) chocolate or rainbow sprinkles

• Cut each banana crosswise in half. Insert wooden stick into each half.

• Pour yogurt into small bowl. Hold banana pop over bowl; spoon yogurt to cover all sides of banana. Allow excess yogurt to drip into bowl. Sprinkle candies over yogurt.

• Place pops on wax paper-lined tray. Freeze 2 hours.

Makes 6 servings

Luau
Fruit Cups

Prep Time: 5 minutes

1 container (6 ounces) piña colada, lemon or vanilla low-fat yogurt
4 waffle cups or cones
2 cups cut-up pineapple, strawberries, mango and green grapes
Ground nutmeg
2 tablespoons flaked coconut, toasted (optional)

Spoon about 1 tablespoon yogurt into each waffle cup. Top each cup evenly with fruit. Spoon remaining yogurt over fruit. Sprinkle with nutmeg. Top with coconut, if desired. Serve immediately.

Makes 4 servings

**Mini Cheese
Burritos (p. 60)**

**Turkey Bacon Mini
Wafflewiches (p. 54)**

Tic-Tac-Toe
Sandwich (p. 52)

Corny Face
(p. 56)

Lunchtime Treats

Earth's Core Meatballs

25 medium to large cherry tomatoes, halved and seeded
3 to 4 ounces part-skim mozzarella cheese, cut into
¼- to ½-inch cubes
2 eggs, divided
2 pounds ground beef
1½ cups Italian-style bread crumbs, divided
1 teaspoon salt
¾ teaspoon garlic powder
½ teaspoon black pepper
Cooked pasta and prepared pasta sauce (optional)

1. Preheat oven to 350°F. Line two baking sheets with foil and spray generously with nonstick cooking spray; set aside.

2. Insert 1 cheese cube into one tomato half; cover with another half to encase cheese.

3. Lightly beat one egg in large bowl. Add beef, ½ cup bread crumbs, salt, garlic powder and pepper; stir until mixed well. Shape 2 tablespoons beef mixture into rough 2-inch circle. Place cheese-filled tomato in center, then bring edges of circle together to completely encase tomato. Lightly roll meatball to form smooth ball. Place on prepared baking sheet. Repeat with remaining meat mixture, tomatoes and cheese.

4. Lightly beat remaining egg in medium shallow bowl. Place 1 cup bread crumbs in another shallow bowl. Dip meatballs one at a time into beaten egg, shake off excess and roll in bread crumbs. Return to baking sheet. Bake 35 minutes until meatballs are slightly crisp and are no longer pink, turning meatballs halfway through baking time. Serve on pasta with sauce, if desired. *Makes 12 servings*

Ham and Potato Pancakes

¾ pound Yukon gold potatoes, peeled, grated and squeezed dry (about 2 cups)
¼ cup finely chopped green onions
2 eggs, beaten
1 cup (4 to 5 ounces) finely chopped cooked ham
¼ cup all-purpose flour
¼ teaspoon salt
¼ teaspoon black pepper
2 to 3 tablespoons vegetable oil
Mild fruit chutney (optional)

1. Combine grated potatoes, green onions and eggs in large bowl; mix well. Add ham, flour, salt and pepper; mix well.

2. Heat 2 tablespoons oil in large heavy-bottomed skillet. Drop batter by heaping tablespoon and press with back of spoon to flatten. Cook over medium-high heat 2 to 3 minutes per side. Remove to paper towels to drain. Add remaining 1 tablespoon oil if necessary to cook remaining batter. Serve pancakes with chutney, if desired.

Makes 4 servings (4 pancakes each)

Sloppy Joe
Race Cars

Prep Time: 25 minutes • **Cook Time:** 20 minutes

1 tablespoon olive oil
1 medium onion, sliced
2 pounds ground turkey or ground beef
1 jar (1 pound 10 ounces) RAGÚ® ROBUSTO!® Pasta Sauce
¼ cup firmly packed brown sugar
2 tablespoons sweet pickle relish
8 hero rolls
   Race Car Garnishes*

For Race Car Garnishes, use mini pretzel twists for steering wheel, zucchini or cucumber slices for wheels attached with thin pretzel or carrot sticks, radish for "driver" with black olives for eyes, carrot sticks for arms, and green pimento-stuffed olives and thinly sliced carrot rounds for headlights.

In 12-inch nonstick skillet, heat olive oil over medium-high heat and cook onion, stirring occasionally, 2 minutes or until tender. Add ground turkey and cook, stirring occasionally, until done.

Stir in Pasta Sauce, brown sugar and relish. Cover and simmer 10 minutes.

Meanwhile, cut out a 5×2-inch *"trench"* in top of rolls, removing some bread. To serve, evenly fill rolls with turkey mixture. Decorate with Race Car Garnishes.   *Makes 8 servings*

Spotted Butterfly Sandwich

Prep Time: 10 minutes

2 slices raisin bread
2 tablespoons cream cheese, softened
1 teaspoon honey
⅛ teaspoon ground cinnamon
1 baby carrot
½ stalk celery
2 carrot strips
2 dried apricots

1. Stack bread slices and cut diagonally into triangles. Place on serving plate with points facing in to form butterfly wings.

2. Combine cream cheese, honey and cinnamon in small bowl. Roll cream cheese mixture into 2 balls and place between bread slices at points, pressing down at points to lift top slice of bread.

3. Place baby carrot in center of bread slices to create body. Cut strips from celery to create antennae. Use carrot strips and apricots to decorate wings.

Makes 1 sandwich

Apple and Cheese Pockets

2 medium to large Golden Delicious apples, peeled, cored and finely chopped (2 cups)
2 cups shredded sharp Cheddar cheese
2 tablespoons apple jelly
¼ teaspoon curry powder
1 package (about 16 ounces) refrigerated reduced-fat large biscuits (8 biscuits)

1. Preheat oven to 350°F. Line baking sheet with parchment paper; set aside.

2. Combine apples, cheese, apple jelly and curry powder in large bowl and stir well.

3. Roll out one biscuit on lightly floured board to 6½-inch circle. Place ½ cup apple mixture in center. Fold biscuit over filling to form a semicircle, and press to seal tightly. Place on baking sheet. Repeat with remaining biscuits and filling. Bake 15 to 18 minutes or until biscuits are golden and filling is hot.

4. To keep hot for lunch, place in vacuum container and close. Or, reheat pockets in microwave about 30 seconds on HIGH until hot.

Makes 8 servings

Note: Refrigerate leftovers up to two days or freeze up to one month.

Tip: Preheat vacuum container with boiling water; drain and dry before use.

Melting
Tuna Calzone

Prep Time: 20 minutes • **Bake Time:** 12 minutes

1 can (6 ounces) tuna packed in water, drained and flaked
½ cup (2 ounces) shredded Cheddar cheese
¼ cup shredded carrot
¼ cup finely chopped celery
3 tablespoons mayonnaise
2 tablespoons sliced green onions
½ teaspoon lemon juice or cider vinegar
¼ teaspoon dried dill weed
⅛ teaspoon pepper
1 package (about 14 ounces) refrigerated pizza crust
Fat-free sour cream
Chopped tomato

1. Preheat oven to 425°F. Lightly coat baking sheet with nonstick cooking spray. Set aside.

2. Combine tuna, cheese, carrot, celery, mayonnaise, green onions, lemon juice, dill weed and pepper in medium bowl .

3. Roll pizza dough into 16½×11-inch rectangle on lightly floured surface. Cut into six squares. Spoon tuna mixture into center of squares.

4. Diagonally fold each square in half, completely enclosing filling. Crimp edges to seal. Place on prepared baking sheet. Bake 12 to 14 minutes or until golden brown. Cool slightly on wire rack. Serve warm with sour cream and tomato.   *Makes 6 servings*

Waffled Grilled Cheese

2 tablespoons butter or margarine
2 slices bread
1 teaspoon mustard
1 slice cheese
1 slice ham

1. Preheat waffle maker. Spread 1 tablespoon butter on one side of each bread slice. Spread mustard on other side of each bread slice. Layer cheese and ham on top of mustard on one bread slice. Top with remaining slice, mustard side down.

2. Spray waffle maker lightly with nonstick cooking spray. Place sandwich in waffle maker; close lid. Cook 3 to 5 minutes or until top is browned and cheese is melted. *Makes 1 serving*

Mucho Gusto Pizza

1 package (11 ounces) refrigerated breadstick dough
1 package (6 ounces) refrigerated grilled chicken breast strips
1 teaspoon chili powder
⅛ teaspoon garlic powder
1 medium tomato, chopped
1 cup (4 ounces) shredded Cheddar cheese
½ cup reduced-fat sour cream
½ cup shredded lettuce

1. Preheat oven to 375°F. Lightly grease baking sheet; set aside.

2. Separate breadstick dough into 4 rectangular portions. On prepared baking sheet press each rectangle into a 5½×4-inch rectangle, pressing perforations together.

3. Combine chicken, chili powder and garlic powder in medium bowl. Arrange chicken pieces and tomato on dough rectangles. Sprinkle with cheese. Bake 15 to 20 minutes or until edges are golden brown. Remove from baking sheet. Top with sour cream and lettuce. *Makes 8 servings*

Focaccia Bars

Cornmeal
1 package (about 11 ounces) refrigerated French bread dough
2 tablespoons olive oil
1 large yellow or red bell pepper, cored and thinly sliced
¼ teaspoon salt
⅛ teaspoon dried oregano
3 tablespoons shredded Italian cheese blend

1. Preheat oven to 400°F. Sprinkle cornmeal on baking sheet. Unwrap bread dough and shape into 16×4-inch strip on prepared baking sheet. Set aside.

2. Heat olive oil in medium skillet over medium-high heat. Add bell pepper; cook and stir 3 to 5 minutes or until pepper is tender and lightly browned. Remove; reserve oil.

3. Press fingertips into dough to create dimples. Drizzle leftover cooking oil from skillet onto dough. Spread pepper slices over dough. Sprinkle with salt and oregano. Top with cheese.

4. Bake 13 to 15 minutes or until cheese melts and bread is firm and golden. Let focaccia rest 2 to 3 minutes. Cut into 4 (4-inch) bars. Serve warm or at room temperature. *Makes 4 servings*

Note: Refrigerate leftovers up to two days or freeze up to one month.

Tic-Tac-Toe Sandwich

Prep Time: 5 minutes

2 teaspoons mayonnaise
1 slice whole wheat bread
1 slice white sandwich bread
1 slice cheese
1 slice deli ham
3 green or black olives

1. Spread 1 teaspoon mayonnaise on each slice of bread. Layer cheese and ham on one bread slice. Top with remaining slice. Trim crust from sandwich. Cut sandwich into 9 squares by cutting into thirds in each direction. Turn alternating pieces over to form checkerboard pattern.

2. Thinly slice 1 olive to form "O"s. Cut remaining 2 olives into strips. Place olive pieces on sandwich squares to form "X"s and "O"s.

Makes 1 sandwich

Turkey Tacos

Prep Time: 10 minutes

1 cup chopped cooked turkey breast or chicken breast
½ cup chopped carrot
⅓ cup chopped celery
¼ cup (1 ounce) shredded taco cheese blend
3 tablespoons mayonnaise
2 tablespoons salsa
6 taco shells

Combine turkey, carrot, celery, cheese, mayonnaise and salsa in medium bowl. Spoon into taco shells.

Makes 6 servings

Turkey Bacon Mini Wafflewiches

1 teaspoon Dijon mustard
1 teaspoon honey
8 frozen mini waffles (2 pieces, divided into individual waffles)
2 thin slices deli turkey, cut into strips
2 tablespoons cooked and crumbled bacon or bacon bits
4 teaspoons shredded Cheddar or mozzarella cheese
2 teaspoons butter

1. Combine mustard and honey in small bowl. Spread small amount of mustard mixture onto 4 waffles. Top each waffle with turkey strips and sprinkle with bacon and cheese. Top with 4 remaining waffles.

2. Melt butter in medium nonstick skillet over medium heat. Cook Wafflewiches 3 to 4 minutes on each side, pressing with back of spatula, until cheese melts and waffles are golden.

Makes 2 servings (2 Wafflewiches each)

Candy Corn by the Slice

1 package (13.8 ounces) refrigerated pizza crust dough
½ cup (2 ounces) shredded mozzarella cheese
2 cups (8 ounces) shredded Cheddar cheese, divided
⅓ cup pizza sauce

1. Preheat oven to 400°F. Spray 13-inch round pizza pan with nonstick cooking spray. Fit pizza dough into pan, shaping as needed.

2. Sprinkle mozzarella in 4-inch circle in center of pizza dough. Sprinkle 1 cup Cheddar cheese in 3-inch ring around center circle; spoon pizza sauce over Cheddar cheese. Create 1½-inch border around edge of pizza with remaining 1 cup Cheddar cheese.

3. Bake 12 to 15 minutes or until edge is lightly browned and cheese is melted and bubbling. Cut into wedges. *Makes 8 slices*

Corny
Face

1 corn tortilla
Nonstick cooking spray
1 slice provolone cheese *or* **3 tablespoons shredded Cheddar cheese**
½ large dill pickle, sliced vertically at an angle
2 slices cucumber
2 pitted black olives
2 tablespoons shredded carrot

1. Heat nonstick skillet over medium heat. Spray skillet lightly with cooking spray. Place tortilla in skillet; top with cheese. Heat 1 minute; fold tortilla in half, enclosing cheese.

2. Cook 1 minute per side or until cheese is melted and tortilla is lightly browned. Place tortilla, rounded side down, on serving plate. Place pickle on top of tortilla at center to resemble nose. Place cucumber slices above tortilla and next to pickle. Top with olives to resemble eyes. Mound carrot over cucumbers to resemble eyebrows. *Makes 1 serving*

Frogs
& Ladybugs

Prep Time: 40 minutes • **Cook Time:** 10 minutes

1 jar (1 pound 10 ounces) RAGÚ® Old World Style® Pasta Sauce

½ cup shredded mozzarella cheese (about 4 ounces)

1 package (12 ounces) refrigerated flaky buttermilk biscuits (10 biscuits)

8 breaded chicken nuggets

Green and red food coloring

1 egg, lightly beaten

Frog and Ladybug Garnishes*

*For Frog & Ladybug Garnishes, use pimiento-stuffed olives for eyes, broccoli for eyebrows, roasted red pepper for mouth, parsley leaves for legs and black olives for spots.

Preheat oven to 400°F. In small bowl, combine ½ cup Pasta Sauce and cheese; set aside.

On lightly floured surface, separate 8 biscuits in half to make 16 rounds. Roll each round into 3½-inch circle. Separate and cut remaining 2 biscuits into 32 pieces; roll into small balls.

On 8 circles, evenly spread sauce mixture leaving ½-inch border; top each with 1 chicken nugget. Press 4 balls onto bottom edges of each circle to create "legs." Top with remaining biscuit circles, sealing edges tightly with fork; set aside.

To color frogs, add 4 drops green food coloring to ½ of the egg, then brush onto ½ of the assembled biscuits. To color ladybugs, add 4 drops red food coloring to remaining egg, then brush onto remaining biscuits.

Bake 10 minutes or until golden. Decorate with Frog and Ladybug Garnishes. Serve with remaining Pasta Sauce, heated.

Makes 8 servings

Mini Cheese Burritos

4 (8-inch) fat-free flour tortillas
½ cup canned fat-free refried beans
½ cup chunky salsa
4 (¾-ounce) reduced-fat Cheddar cheese sticks*

*Reduced-fat Cheddar cheese block can be substituted. Cut cheese into 2×¼×¼-inch sticks.

1. Spread beans over tortillas, leaving ½-inch border around edges. Spoon salsa over beans.

2. Place cheese stick on one side of each tortilla. Fold one edge of each tortilla over cheese stick; roll up. Place burritos, seam side down, on microwavable dish.

3. Microwave on HIGH 1 to 2 minutes or until cheese is melted. Let stand 1 to 2 minutes before serving.   *Makes 4 servings*

Sammich Swirls

1 package (11 ounces) refrigerated French bread dough
Salt-free seasoning mix (optional)
Yellow mustard
4 slices light bologna
4 slices reduced-fat provolone cheese
2 teaspoons grated Parmesan cheese

1. Preheat oven to 350°F. Roll out bread dough to 10×12-inch rectangle. Sprinkle with seasoning, if desired. Dot with mustard.

2. Arrange bologna and cheese, alternating and overlapping edges to cover dough. Roll up lengthwise like a jelly roll; pinch seams to seal. Place dough, seam side down, on baking sheet. Sprinkle with Parmesan cheese.

3. Bake 25 to 30 minutes or until puffy and browned. Let cool. Cut into 1-inch slices. *Makes 10 slices*

Crescent Moons

Prep Time: 10 minutes • **Bake Time:** 11 minutes

1 package (8 ounces) refrigerated reduced-fat crescent
roll dough
½ cup finely chopped ham
½ cup shredded Cheddar cheese
2 tablespoons sliced green onions
Pizza sauce or honey-mustard salad dressing

1. Preheat oven to 375°F. Separate dough into 8 triangles.

2. Sprinkle triangles with ham, cheese and green onions. Starting at the large end, loosely roll-up toward point. Curve to form crescent shape. Place on ungreased baking sheet. Bake 11 to 13 minutes or until golden brown.

3. Serve warm with pizza sauce. *Makes 8 servings*

Inside-Out
Breadsticks

**1 package (about 11 ounces) refrigerated breadsticks
   (12 breadsticks)**
1 package (8 ounces) reduced-fat cream cheese, softened
1 to 2 tablespoons milk
¼ cup finely chopped carrot
2 tablespoons minced chives or green onions
12 slices deli ham, roast beef, turkey or chicken

1. Bake breadsticks according to package directions; cool.

2. Beat cream cheese with enough milk to make mixture spreadable. Stir
in carrot and chives. Spread 1 rounded tablespoon cream cheese mixture
over ham slice. Roll ham slice around breadstick. Repeat with remaining
breadsticks. Wrap tightly in plastic wrap. Refrigerate until ready to serve or
pack in lunchbox.   *Makes 6 servings*

Note: Wrap and freeze leftover breadsticks. Cream cheese spread may be
refrigerated up to two days.

Tip: To keep breadsticks cool in the lunchbox, include a frozen juice box
or frozen gel pack. Tell your kids to throw away leftovers.

Peanutty Ham Turnovers

8 ounces finely diced cooked ham (about 2 cups)
1 cup (4 ounces) shredded Monterey Jack cheese
¼ cup chopped roasted salted peanuts
3 tablespoons orange marmalade
2 tablespoons dried currants
1 to 1¼ teaspoons chili powder
1 package (about 16 ounces) refrigerated reduced-fat large biscuits (8 biscuits)

1. Preheat oven to 350°F. Line baking sheet with parchment paper; set aside.

2. Combine ham, cheese, peanuts, marmalade, currants and chili powder, to taste, in bowl. Stir well.

3. Roll out each biscuit to 6-inch diameter on lightly floured board. Divide filling evenly, spooning about ⅓ cup into center of each biscuit. Fold biscuit over filling to form a semicircle, and press to seal tightly. Place on baking sheet. Bake 15 minutes or until biscuits are golden and filling is hot. *Makes 8 servings*

Note: Refrigerate extra turnovers up to two days or freeze up to one month. Place in individual resealable plastic food storage bags for storage and packing.

Tip: The turnovers are good hot or cold. To keep turnovers cool in the lunchbox, include a frozen juice box or frozen gel pack. Reheat in microwave, if desired. Tell your kids to throw away leftovers.

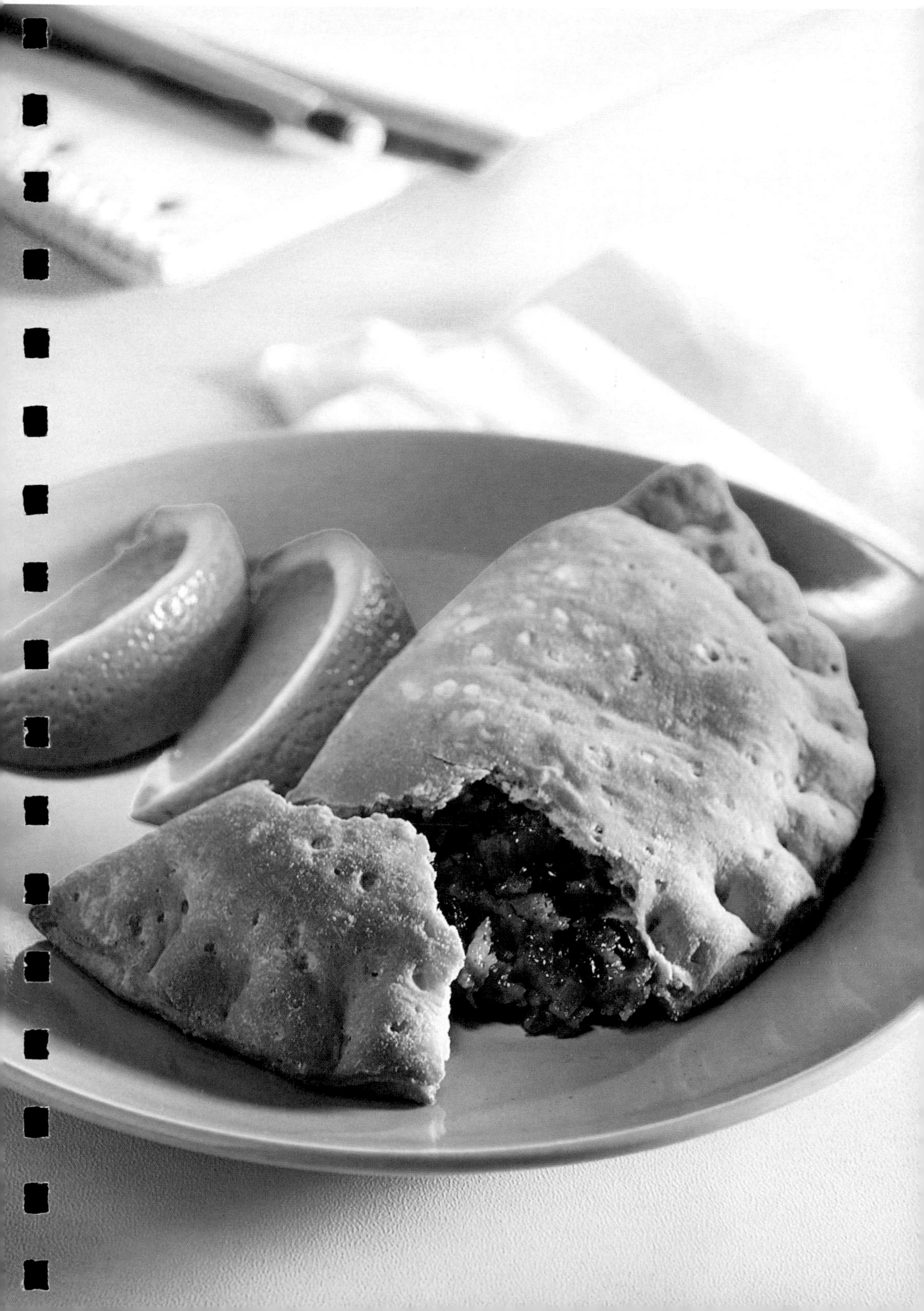

**Bear Bite Snack
Mix (p. 82)**

**Doodle Bug
Cupcakes (p. 88)**

Cheddar Broccoli
Martians (p. 92)

Pretty Pink
Pies (p. 74)

Party Time

Double Chocolate Chip Snack Cake

1 package (18¼ ounces) devil's food cake mix with pudding in the mix, divided
2 eggs
½ cup water
¼ cup vegetable oil
½ teaspoon cinnamon
1 cup semisweet chocolate chips, divided
¼ cup packed brown sugar
2 tablespoons butter, melted
¾ cup white chocolate chips

1. Preheat oven to 350°F. Grease 9-inch round cake pan. Reserve ¾ cup cake mix; set aside.

2. Pour remaining cake mix into large bowl. Add eggs, water, oil and cinnamon; beat with electric mixer at medium speed 2 minutes. Remove ½ cup batter; reserve for another use.* Spread remaining batter in prepared pan; sprinkle with ½ cup semisweet chocolate chips.

3. Combine reserved cake mix and brown sugar in medium bowl. Stir in butter and remaining ½ cup semisweet chocolate chips; mix well. Sprinkle mixture over batter in pan.

4. Bake 35 to 40 minutes or until toothpick inserted into center comes out clean and cake springs back when lightly touched.

5. Place white chocolate chips in resealable food storage bag; seal bag. Microwave on HIGH 10 seconds and knead bag gently. Repeat until chips are melted. Cut off ¼ inch from corner of bag with scissors; drizzle chocolate over cake. Cool cake on wire rack before cutting into wedges.

Makes 8 to 10 servings

If desired, extra batter can be used for cupcakes: Pour batter into two foil or paper cupcake liners placed on baking sheet; bake at 350°F 20 to 25 minutes or until toothpick inserted into centers comes out clean.

Funny Face Cheese Ball

Prep Time: 15 minutes

2 packages (8 ounces each) reduced-fat cream cheese, softened
2 cups (8 ounces) shredded Mexican cheese blend
1¼ cups shredded carrots, divided
2 tablespoons fat-free (skim) milk
2 teaspoons chili powder
¼ teaspoon ground cumin
¼ teaspoon garlic powder
1 pimiento-stuffed green olive, sliced
1 peperoncini pepper
Red or yellow bell pepper pieces
Reduced-fat shredded wheat crackers or celery sticks

1. Beat cream cheese, cheese, 1 cup shredded carrots, milk, chili powder, cumin and garlic powder in large bowl with electric mixer at medium speed until well blended.

2. Shape mixture into ball. Arrange remaining ¼ cup shredded carrot on top of ball for hair. Use olive slices for eyes, peperoncini pepper for nose and bell pepper for ears and mouth.

3. Serve immediately or cover and refrigerate until serving time. Serve with crackers or celery sticks.

Makes 24 servings (2 tablespoons cheese mixture plus 4 crackers)

Pretty
Pink Pies

1 small ripe banana, sliced
1 package (4 ounces) mini graham cracker crumb pie crusts (6 crusts)
2 tablespoons chocolate ice cream topping
2 containers (6 ounces each) strawberry low-fat yogurt
6 miniature pastel marshmallows or miniature marshmallows
6 medium fresh strawberries, cut into wedges

1. Place banana slices in each pie crust. Drizzle with 1 teaspoon chocolate topping. Spoon yogurt over top.

2. Place 1 marshmallow in the center of each pie. Arrange strawberry pieces around marshmallow to resemble flower. Serve immediately or cover and refrigerate up to 4 hours. *Makes 6 servings*

Meteorite Mini Cakes

1 package (18¼ ounces) chocolate cake mix, plus ingredients to prepare mix
2 containers (16 ounces each) vanilla frosting, divided
Assorted food coloring
1 bag (11 ounces) chocolate baking chunks

1. Preheat oven to 350°F. Spray 12 standard (2½-inch) muffin pan cups with nonstick cooking spray. Prepare cake mix according to package directions. Divide batter evenly among muffin cups. Bake 20 to 25 minutes or until toothpick inserted into centers comes out clean. Cool 5 minutes on wire rack; remove from pan and cool completely.

2. Use kitchen shears to trim cupcake edges and form rounded, irregular shapes. Place 2 cups frosting in microwavable bowl and heat on LOW (30%), until melted, about 30 seconds. Tint as desired with food coloring. Stir until smooth. Drizzle frosting over cupcakes, coating completely.

3. Chill cakes 20 minutes. Dot cakes with chocolate baking chunks to make meteorite surface. Melt and tint remaining frosting as desired and coat baking chunks with frosting. Chill until ready to serve. *Makes 12 servings*

S'mores
on a Stick

Prep Time: 10 minutes • **Cook Time:** 3 minutes

1 (14-ounce) can EAGLE BRAND® Sweetened Condensed Milk (NOT evaporated milk), divided
1½ cups mini milk chocolate chips, divided
1 cup miniature marshmallows
11 whole graham crackers, halved crosswise
Toppings: chopped peanuts, miniature candy-coated chocolate pieces, sprinkles

1. In microwave-safe bowl, microwave half of EAGLE BRAND® at HIGH (100% power) 1½ minutes. Stir in 1 cup chocolate chips until smooth; stir in marshmallows.

2. Spread chocolate mixture evenly by heaping tablespoonfuls onto 11 graham cracker halves. Top with remaining graham cracker halves; place on wax paper.

3. Microwave remaining EAGLE BRAND® at HIGH (100% power) 1½ minutes; stir in remaining ½ cup chocolate chips, stirring until smooth. Drizzle mixture over treats; sprinkle with desired toppings.

4. Let stand for 2 hours; insert wooden craft stick into center of each treat. *Makes 11 servings*

Mysterious
Colorful Jiggles

1 package (4-serving size) lime gelatin or flavor of your choice
1 package (4-serving size) orange gelatin or flavor of your choice
1 package (4-serving size) blue raspberry gelatin or flavor of your choice
Whipped topping
Colored sprinkles

1. Prepare lime gelatin according to package directions and place in small pitcher or 2-cup measuring cup. Pour ¼ cup lime gelatin mixture into each of 8 (8- to 10-ounce) clear plastic cups. Refrigerate 2 hours or until gelatin is firm.

2. Meanwhile, prepare orange gelatin according to package directions and place in small pitcher or 2-cup measuring cup. Refrigerate 1 hour or until gelatin just begins to gel.

3. Remove lime gelatin cups from refrigerator. Pour ¼ cup orange gelatin into cups and refrigerate until firm; about 2 hours.

4. Meanwhile, prepare blue raspberry gelatin according to package directions and place in small pitcher or 2-cup measuring cup. Refrigerate 1 hour or until gelatin just begins to gel.

5. Remove gelatin cups from refrigerator. Pour ¼ cup blue raspberry gelatin into cups and refrigerate until firm; about 2 hours.

6. Serve with whipped topping and sprinkles.   *Makes 8 servings*

Pizza Dippin' Strips

Prep Time: 10 minutes • **Cook Time:** 15 minutes

1 package (13.8 ounces) refrigerated pizza crust dough
15 thin slices pepperoni
1 cup shredded mozzarella cheese (about 4 ounces)
1 jar (1 pound 10 ounces) RAGÚ® Organic Pasta Sauce, heated

1. Preheat oven to 400°F.

2. On greased baking sheet, roll pizza dough into 12×9-inch rectangle. Fold edges over to make ¾-inch crust. Bake 7 minutes.

3. Evenly top pizza crust with pepperoni, then cheese. Bake an additional 8 minutes or until cheese is melted. Let stand 2 minutes.

4. Cut pizza in half lengthwise, then into 1½-inch strips. Serve with Pasta Sauce, heated, for dipping.   *Makes 16 strips*

"M&M's"® Family Party Mix

2 tablespoons butter or margarine*
¼ cup honey*
2 cups favorite grain cereal or 3 cups granola
1 cup coarsely chopped nuts
1 cup thin pretzel pieces
1 cup raisins
2 cups "M&M's"® Chocolate Mini Baking Bits

*For a drier mix, eliminate butter and honey. Simply combine dry ingredients and do not bake.

Preheat oven to 300°F. In large saucepan over low heat, melt butter; add honey and stir until well blended. Remove from heat and add cereal, nuts, pretzel pieces and raisins, stirring until all pieces are evenly coated. Spread mixture onto ungreased cookie sheet and bake about 10 minutes. Do not overbake. Spread mixture onto waxed paper and allow to cool completely. In large bowl combine mixture and "M&M's"® Chocolate Mini Baking Bits. Store in tightly covered container.   *Makes about 6 cups snack mix*

Bear Bite
Snack Mix

   2 teaspoons sugar
   ¾ teaspoon ground cinnamon
   ¼ teaspoon ground nutmeg
 1½ cups sweetened corn or oat cereal squares
   1 cup raisins
   1 cup teddy bear-shaped cookies
   ½ cup dried fruit bits or chopped mixed dried fruit
      Nonstick cooking spray

1. Preheat oven to 350°F. Combine sugar, cinnamon and nutmeg in small bowl; mix well.

2. Combine cereal, raisins, cookies and dried fruit in large bowl. Spread on jelly-roll pan. Generously spray with cooking spray. Sprinkle with half sugar mixture. Stir well. Spray again with cooking spray; sprinkle with remaining sugar mixture.

3. Bake 5 minutes; stir. Bake 5 minutes more; stir. Cool completely in pan on wire rack. Store in airtight container.   *Makes 4 cups snack mix*

Fun Fruit Kabobs

   4 small strawberries (or 2 large strawberries cut in half
      lengthwise) with green leaves removed
   4 banana slices (¼ of small banana)
   4 green grapes
   4 (2¼-inch) pretzel sticks

1. Gently push 1 strawberry, 1 banana slice and 1 grape onto each pretzel stick. Twist pretzel while pushing fruit onto it to keep the pretzel from breaking.

2. Serve immediately or pretzels may become soggy.   *Makes 1 serving*

Bedrock
Fruit Boulders

Prep Time: 20 minutes • **Bake Time:** 16 minutes

1 package (about 16 ounces) refrigerated large buttermilk biscuits (8 biscuits)
1¼ cups finely chopped apple (about 1 small apple)
⅓ cup dried mixed fruit bits
2 tablespoons packed brown sugar
½ teaspoon ground cinnamon
1 cup sifted powdered sugar
4 to 5 teaspoons orange juice

1. Preheat oven to 350°F. Line baking sheet with parchment paper or lightly spray with nonstick cooking spray. Set aside.

2. Cut each biscuit in half horizontally, making 16 rounds. Roll each round into 3½-inch circle.

3. Combine apple, dried fruit, brown sugar and cinnamon in small bowl. Spoon 1 rounded tablespoon apple mixture into center of each circle. Moisten edges of dough with water. Pull dough up and around filling, completely enclosing filling. Pinch edges to seal.

4. Place rolls, seam side down, on prepared baking sheet. Bake 16 to 18 minutes or until golden brown. Cool 10 minutes on wire rack.

5. Combine powdered sugar and enough orange juice to make mixture of drizzling consistency in small bowl. Spoon over rolls. Serve warm.

Makes 16 servings

Clown-Around
Cones

4 waffle cones
½ cup "M&M's"® Chocolate Mini Baking Bits, divided
 Prepared decorator icing
½ cup hot fudge ice cream topping, divided
4 cups any flavor ice cream, softened
1 (1.5- to 2-ounce) chocolate candy bar, chopped
¼ cup caramel ice cream topping

Decorate cones as desired with "M&M's"® Chocolate Mini Baking Bits, using decorator icing to attach; let set. For each cone, place 1 tablespoon hot fudge topping in bottom of cone. Sprinkle with 1 teaspoon "M&M's"® Chocolate Mini Baking Bits. Layer with ¼ cup ice cream; sprinkle with ¼ of candy bar. Layer with ¼ cup ice cream; sprinkle with 1 teaspoon "M&M's"® Chocolate Mini Baking Bits. Top with 1 tablespoon caramel topping and remaining ½ cup ice cream. Wrap in plastic wrap and freeze until ready to serve. Just before serving, top each ice cream cone with 1 tablespoon hot fudge topping; sprinkle with remaining "M&M's"® Chocolate Mini Baking Bits. Serve immediately. *Makes 4 servings*

Doodle Bug Cupcakes

1 package (18¼ ounces) white cake mix *without* pudding in the mix
1 cup sour cream
3 eggs
⅓ cup vegetable oil
⅓ cup water
1 teaspoon vanilla
1½ cups prepared cream cheese frosting
   Red, yellow, blue and green food coloring
   Red licorice strings, cut into 2-inch pieces
   Assorted round decorating candies

1. Preheat oven to 350°F. Line 24 standard (2½-inch) muffin pan cups with paper baking cups.

2. Beat cake mix, sour cream, eggs, oil, water and vanilla in large bowl with electric mixer at low speed about 1 minute or until blended. Increase speed to medium; beat 1 to 2 minutes or until smooth.

3. Fill muffin cups about two-thirds full. Bake about 20 minutes or until toothpick inserted into centers comes out clean. Cool cupcakes in pans on wire racks 5 minutes; remove from pans and cool completely.

4. Divide frosting evenly between 4 small bowls. Add food coloring to each bowl, one drop at a time, to reach desired shades; stir each frosting until well blended. Frost tops of cupcakes.

5. Use toothpick to make three small holes on opposite sides of each cupcake, making 6 holes total. Insert licorice piece into each hole for legs. Decorate tops of cupcakes with assorted candies.   *Makes 24 cupcakes*

Cherry Tomato Planets

1 bag (20 ounces) cherry tomatoes
¼ cup (1 ounce) shredded mozzarella cheese
20 slices pepperoni

1. Preheat broiler. Slice ⅛ inch off stem end of tomatoes using paring knife; reserve tops. Core tomatoes using small melon baller or by carefully pinching out core using thumb and index finger.

2. Fill each tomato with cheese; top with slice of pepperoni. Cover with reserved tomato top; secure with toothpick.

3. Place filled tomatoes on baking sheet. Broil about 6 inches from heat source for 3 minutes or until cheese is melted and tomatoes just begin to shrivel.

4. Transfer tomatoes to paper towel-lined plate to drain. Remove toothpicks before serving. Serve warm.   *Makes about 20 appetizers*

Baked Taco Chicken Bites

1 egg white, beaten
1 tablespoon water
1 package (about 1 ounce) reduced-sodium taco seasoning
¼ cup yellow cornmeal
2 tablespoons all-purpose flour
1 pound boneless skinless chicken breasts
2 tablespoons butter or margarine, melted
   Ranch salad dressing or spicy ranch salad dressing

1. Preheat oven to 450°F. Grease baking sheet. Set aside. Combine egg white and water in shallow dish. Combine taco seasoning, cornmeal and flour in another shallow dish.

2. Cut chicken into 1½- to 2-inch pieces. Dip chicken pieces into egg white mixture. Roll in crumb mixture. Place in single layer on prepared baking sheet. Drizzle with melted butter. Bake 11 to 13 minutes or until chicken is no longer pink in center.

3. Serve with salad dressing as dipping sauce.   *Makes 6 to 8 servings*

Cheddar Broccoli Martians

Prep Time: 25 minutes • **Cook Time:** 10 minutes

1 package (10 ounces) frozen chopped broccoli, thawed
1 jar (1 pound) RAGÚ® Cheesy! Double Cheddar Sauce,
    divided
2 tablespoons Italian seasoned dry bread crumbs
1 package (12 ounces) refrigerated flaky buttermilk
    biscuits (10 biscuits)
    Green food coloring
1 egg
    Martian Garnishes*

*For Martian Garnishes, use thinly sliced carrot rounds and peas for eyes, broccoli for nose and eyebrows and chow mein noodles for antenna and mouth.

Preheat oven to 400°F. Arrange broccoli on double layer of paper towels and squeeze dry. In small bowl, combine broccoli, ¾ cup Double Cheddar Sauce and bread crumbs; set aside.

Separate biscuits in half to make 20 pieces. On lightly floured surface, roll each into a 3½-inch circle. On ungreased baking sheet, arrange 10 biscuit circles. Evenly spread 10 circles with broccoli mixture leaving ½-inch border. Top with remaining biscuit circles, sealing edges tightly with fork. Beat 4 drops food coloring with egg, then brush on circles.

Bake 10 minutes or until golden. Decorate with Martian Garnishes. Serve with remaining Double Cheddar Sauce, heated.   *Makes 10 servings*

Cookie
Pizza Cake

1 package (18 ounces) refrigerated chocolate chip cookie
dough
1 package (18¼ ounces) chocolate cake mix, plus
ingredients to prepare mix
1 cup prepared vanilla frosting
½ cup peanut butter
1 to 2 tablespoons milk
1 container (16 ounces) chocolate frosting
Chocolate peanut butter cups, chopped (optional)

1. Preheat oven to 350°F. Coat two 12×1-inch round pizza pans with nonstick cooking spray. Press cookie dough evenly into one pan. Bake 15 to 20 minutes or until edges are golden brown. Cool 20 minutes in pan on wire rack. Remove from pan; cool completely on wire rack.

2. Prepare cake mix according to package directions. Fill second pan one-quarter to half full with batter. (Reserve remaining cake batter for another use, such as cupcakes.) Bake 10 to 15 minutes or until toothpick inserted into center comes out clean. Cool 15 minutes on wire rack. Gently remove cake from pan; cool completely.

3. Combine vanilla frosting and peanut butter in small bowl. Gradually stir in milk, 1 tablespoon at a time, until mixture is of spreadable consistency.

4. Place cookie on serving plate. Spread peanut butter frosting over cookie. Place cake on top of cookie, trimming cookie to match the size of cake, if necessary. Frost top and side of cake with chocolate frosting. Garnish with peanut butter cups, if desired.   *Makes 12 to 14 servings*

You Make Me Dizzy Sub

Prep Time: 15 minutes • **Bake Time:** 25 minutes

2 packages (11 ounces each) refrigerated French bread dough
⅓ cup Italian vinaigrette salad dressing
  Lettuce leaves
6 ounces thinly sliced ham
6 ounces thinly sliced cooked chicken breast or turkey breast
2 ounces thinly sliced hard salami
6 ounces thinly sliced Cheddar cheese, Monterey Jack cheese or combination
1 can (2¼ ounces) sliced pitted ripe olives, drained
2 small tomatoes, thinly sliced

1. Preheat oven to 350°F. Lightly spray 12-inch pizza pan or baking sheet with nonstick cooking spray. Place dough on prepared pan, seam side down. Pinch ends of dough together to form one 10-inch ring. Cut shallow diagonal slices in top of dough. Bake 25 to 30 minutes or until golden brown. Remove to wire rack. Cool completely.

2. Horizontally slice loaf in half using serrated knife. Drizzle bottom of loaf with salad dressing. Layer lettuce leaves, ham, chicken, salami and cheese on bottom of loaf. Sprinkle with olives. Top with tomatoes. Cover with top of loaf. Cut into wedges to serve. *Makes 12 servings*

Pizza Fondue

Prep Time: 15 minutes • **Cook Time:** 3 to 4 hours

½ pound bulk Italian sausage
1 cup chopped onion
2 jars (26 ounces each) meatless pasta sauce
4 ounces thinly sliced ham, finely chopped
1 package (3 ounces) sliced pepperoni, finely chopped
1 pound mozzarella cheese, cut into ¾-inch cubes
1 loaf Italian or French bread, cut into 1-inch cubes

Slow Cooker Directions

1. Cook sausage and onion in large skillet over medium-high heat, until sausage is browned, stirring to break up meat. Drain fat. Transfer sausage mixture to slow cooker.

2. Stir in pasta sauce, ham and pepperoni. Cover; cook on LOW 3 to 4 hours.

3. Serve fondue with cheese and bread cubes.

Makes 20 to 25 servings

Gooey Coconut Chocolate Cupcakes

1 package (18¼ ounces) chocolate cake mix, plus ingredients to prepare mix
½ cup (1 stick) butter or margarine
1 cup brown sugar
⅓ cup cream, half-and-half or milk
1½ cups sweetened flaked coconut
½ cup chopped pecans (optional)

1. Preheat oven to 350°F. Line 24 standard (2½-inch) muffin pan cups with foil baking cups. Prepare cake mix according to package directions. Fill prepared muffin cups about half full. Bake 18 minutes or until toothpick inserted into centers comes out clean. Do not remove cupcakes from pan.

2. Meanwhile, melt butter in a medium saucepan over low heat. Stir in brown sugar and cream until well blended and sugar is dissolved. Add coconut and pecans, if desired; mix well.

3. Spread 2 to 3 tablespoons brown sugar mixture over each cupcake. Place cupcakes under preheated broiler 2 to 3 minutes or until tops begin to brown and bubble around the edges. Serve warm or cool.

Makes 24 cupcakes

Veggie Pizza Pitas

Prep Time: 10 minutes

2 rounds whole wheat pita bread, cut in half horizontally (to make 4 rounds)
¼ cup pizza sauce
1 teaspoon dried basil
⅛ teaspoon red pepper flakes (optional)
1 cup sliced mushrooms
½ cup thinly sliced green bell pepper
½ cup thinly sliced red onion
1 cup (4 ounces) shredded mozzarella cheese
2 teaspoons grated Parmesan cheese

1. Preheat oven to 475°F.

2. Arrange pita rounds, rough sides up, in single layer on large nonstick baking sheet. Spread 1 tablespoon pizza sauce evenly over each round to within ¼ inch of edge. Sprinkle with basil and red pepper flakes, if desired. Top with mushrooms, bell pepper and onion. Sprinkle with mozzarella.

3. Bake 5 minutes or until cheese is melted and pita edges are golden brown. Remove from oven. Sprinkle ½ teaspoon Parmesan over each round. *Makes 4 servings*

Cherry Tomato Pops (p. 110)

Fish Biters (p. 124)

Jungle Juice
(p. 116)

Cinnamon Toast
Poppers (p. 120)

Afternoon **Nibbles**

Popcorn Truffles

8 cups popped plain popcorn
2 cups (12 ounces) semisweet chocolate chips
   Colored sprinkles (optional)

1. Line 2 baking sheets with waxed paper. Place popcorn in large bowl.

2. Place chocolate chips in microwavable bowl. Microwave on HIGH 30 seconds; stir. Repeat, if necessary, until chips are melted. Pour over popcorn; stir until well coated.

3. Scoop popcorn mixture with small ice cream scoop, pressing mixture slightly against the inside of bowl. Drop by scoopfuls onto prepared baking sheets. Decorate with sprinkles, if desired. Allow to harden at room temperature or refrigerate. Store truffles in air-tight container up to 3 days.   *Makes 40 (1½-inch) truffles*

Ticos Fricos

1 container (6 ounces) shredded Parmesan cheese
   Nonstick cooking spray
   Salsa or bean dip

1. Heat medium nonstick skillet over medium heat. Lightly spray with cooking spray. Sprinkle 2 to 3 tablespoons cheese in bottom of pan in light, even layer, creating circular pattern.

2. Cook 2 to 3 minutes or until edges and bottom are evenly browned. Carefully turn frico over with edge of spatula; cook about 30 seconds longer.

3. Remove frico from pan and place on paper towel to cool. (Frico may cool over back of a custard cup or over rolling pin if a shape is desired.) Frico will be crisp when cool. Serve with salsa or bean dip.
Makes about 12 fricos

Cheesy Snails

1 package (about 12 ounces) refrigerated French bread dough
5 part-skim mozzarella string cheese sticks
1 egg
1 tablespoon heavy cream
2 tablespoons sesame seeds

1. Preheat oven to 350°F. Line baking sheets with parchment paper.

2. Roll out bread dough into 12×10-inch rectangle and cut in half lengthwise to make two 10×6-inch sheets. Cut each sheet into five 6×2-inch rectangles.

3. Slice cheese stick in half lengthwise. Crimp piece of dough around each piece of cheese, leaving one-quarter inch of cheese exposed at end. Beginning with other end, roll into coil shape to make snail. Place on prepared baking sheets.

4. Beat egg and cream in small bowl. Brush dough coils with egg mixture and sprinkle with sesame seeds. Bake 20 to 25 minutes or until dough is browned and cheese oozes. Cool slightly before serving.

Makes 10 servings

Pretzel
Fried Eggs

24 (1-inch) pretzel rings
1 cup white chocolate chips
24 yellow candy-coated chocolate pieces

1. Line baking sheet with waxed paper. Place pretzel rings on prepared baking sheet about 2 inches apart.

2. Place white chocolate chips in 1-quart resealable food storage bag; seal bag. Microwave on HIGH 30 seconds. Knead bag gently and microwave 30 seconds more; repeat until chips are melted. Cut ¼-inch corner from bag.

3. Squeeze chocolate from bag onto each pretzel ring in circular motion. Fill center of pretzel first and finish with ring of chocolate around edge of pretzel. Use tip of small knife to smooth chocolate, if necessary. Place candy piece in center of each pretzel. Allow to harden at room temperature or refrigerate until set. Store in single layer in air-tight container up to one week. *Makes 24 eggs*

Cherry Tomato Pops

4 part-skim mozzarella string cheese sticks (1 ounce each)
8 cherry tomatoes
3 tablespoons fat-free ranch dressing

1. Slice cheese sticks in half lengthwise. Trim stem end of each cherry tomato and remove pulp and seeds.

2. Press end of string cheese into hollowed tomato to make cherry tomato pop. Serve with ranch dressing for dipping. *Makes 8 pops*

Granola Sunshine

Prep Time: 20 minutes

1 bag (10 ounces) marshmallows
¼ cup (½ stick) butter or margarine
3 cups granola
3 cups crisp rice cereal
  Prepared white frosting
  Dried pineapple
  Yellow food coloring

1. Line 13×9-inch baking pan with foil. Lightly spray foil with nonstick cooking spray. Set aside.

2. Combine marshmallows and butter in large saucepan. Cook and stir over low heat until marshmallows melt. Stir in granola and cereal.

3. Pat mixture into prepared pan. Let stand at least 30 minutes. Use cookie cutter to cut into 2½-inch circles. Use frosting to attach dried pineapple wedges around edges of circle to resemble rays of sun. Combine some of remaining frosting and food coloring in small bowl until desired shade is reached. Draw eyes, nose and mouth with frosting in center of each sun. *Makes 12 servings*

Chocolate
Panini Bites

¼ cup chocolate hazelnut spread
4 slices good-quality sandwich bread or Italian bread

1. Preheat indoor grill.* Spread chocolate hazelnut spread evenly over two slices bread; top with remaining slices.

2. Spray sandwiches lightly with nonstick cooking spray. Grill 2 to 3 minutes or until bread is golden brown. Cut sandwiches into triangles.

Makes 4 servings

*Panini can also be made on the stove on a ridged grill pan or in a nonstick skillet. Cook sandwiches over medium heat about 2 minutes per side.

Chocolate Raspberry Panini Bites: Spread 2 slices bread with raspberry jam or preserves; spread remaining slices with chocolate hazelnut spread. Cook sandwiches as directed above; watch grill or pan closely because jam burns easily.

Chunky Chews

Prep Time: 20 minutes

1 cup powdered sugar, divided
½ cup chunky peanut butter
2 tablespoons honey
2 tablespoons raisins
2 tablespoons coconut, plus additional for coating
2 tablespoons chopped nuts

1. Combine ½ cup powdered sugar, peanut butter and honey in medium bowl. Mix until well blended. (Mixture may be crumbly.) Add raisins and coconut; mix well. Form dough into ¾ inch balls.

2. Coat balls in remaining ½ cup powdered sugar, additional coconut, chopped nuts or leave plain. Place chews in paper candy wrappers, if desired. To store, place in airtight container up to 4 days.

Makes about 3 dozen chews

Give Me S'more Muffins

Prep Time: 25 minutes

2 cups graham cracker crumbs
⅓ cup sugar
2 teaspoons baking powder
⅓ cup mini chocolate chips
1 egg
¾ cup milk
24 milk chocolate candy kisses, unwrapped
2 cups mini marshmallows

1. Preheat oven to 350°F. Line mini (1¾-inch) muffin cups with paper baking cups. Set aside.

2. Combine graham cracker crumbs, sugar, baking powder and mini chips in medium bowl. Whisk egg into milk and stir into crumb mixture until well blended.

3. Spoon batter into prepared pan, filling each cup about half full. Press chocolate kiss into each cup. Press 4 marshmallows into tops of each muffin. Bake 10 to 12 minutes or until marshmallows are lightly browned. Cool 10 minutes in pan before removing to wire rack to cool.

Makes about 2 dozen mini muffins

Jungle Juice

1 banana
1 cup frozen strawberries
1 container (6 ounces) vanilla low-fat yogurt
2 tablespoons frozen orange juice concentrate
2 tablespoons strawberry syrup
   Fresh orange slices, optional

1. Place banana, strawberries, yogurt and frozen orange juice concentrate in blender. Blend until smooth, scraping down sides of blender as needed.

2. Evenly drizzle syrup around inside of 2 tall, clear glasses. Pour Jungle Juice into glasses. Garnish with orange slices.   *Makes 2 servings*

Twisted Dunkers

Prep Time: 15 minutes • **Bake Time:** 15 minutes

¾ cup finely grated Parmesan cheese
½ teaspoon dried oregano
¼ teaspoon garlic powder
1 egg, beaten
1 tablespoon water
1 package (11 ounces) refrigerated breadstick dough
¾ cup pizza sauce

1. Preheat oven to 375°F. Grease large baking sheet; set aside.

2. Combine Parmesan, oregano and garlic powder in shallow dish. Combine egg and water in another shallow dish.

3. Unroll breadstick dough. Separate into 12 pieces. Dip each breadstick in egg mixture. Roll in Parmesan mixture. Twist each breadstick twice. Place on prepared baking sheet. Bake 12 minutes or until golden brown.

4. Meanwhile, heat pizza sauce in small microwavable bowl on HIGH 15 seconds or until warm. Serve warm breadsticks with warm pizza sauce.
Makes 6 servings (2 breadsticks each)

Caramel
Popcorn Balls

16 cups plain popped popcorn (do not use buttered popcorn)
1 package (14 ounces) caramels
¼ cup (½ stick) butter
Pinch of salt
1⅔ cups shredded coconut
1 package (12 ounces) semisweet chocolate chips
10 to 12 lollipop sticks
Halloween sprinkles and decorations (optional)

1. Place popcorn in large bowl.

2. Place caramels and butter in medium saucepan over low heat. Cook and stir until caramels and butter are melted and smooth, about 5 minutes. Stir in salt and coconut. Remove caramel mixture from heat; pour over popcorn. With large wooden spoon, mix until popcorn is evenly coated. Let cool slightly.

3. Place chocolate chips in microwavable bowl. Microwave on HIGH 1 minute; stir. Microwave on HIGH for additional 30-second intervals until chips are completely melted, stirring after each 30-second interval. Stir until smooth.

4. When popcorn mixture is cool enough to handle, grease hands with butter or nonstick cooking spray. Shape popcorn mixture into baseball-sized balls; place 1 lollipop stick in each ball. Dip bottom of each popcorn ball into melted chocolate and roll in Halloween decorations, if desired. Place on waxed paper until chocolate is set.   *Makes 10 to 12 balls*

Variation: Pour melted chocolate over caramel popcorn mixture; mix by hand until popcorn is coated with chocolate. Spread evenly on baking sheet lined with waxed paper until chocolate is set. Serve as a snack mix.

Cinnamon Toast Poppers

2 tablespoons butter
6 cups fresh bread* cubes (1-inch cubes)
1 tablespoon plus 1½ teaspoons sugar
½ teaspoon ground cinnamon

*Use a firm sourdough, whole wheat or semolina bread.

1. Preheat oven to 325°F. Melt butter in Dutch oven or large skillet over low heat. Add bread cubes and toss to coat; remove from heat. Combine sugar and cinnamon in small bowl. Sprinkle over bread cubes; stir well.

2. Spread bread cubes in one layer on ungreased baking sheet. Bake 25 minutes or until bread is golden and fragrant, stirring once or twice. Serve warm or at room temperature.   *Makes 12 servings*

Crisp Tortellini Bites

Prep Time: 15 minutes • **Total Time:** 30 minutes

½ cup plain dry bread crumbs
¼ cup grated Parmesan cheese
2 teaspoons HERB-OX® chicken flavored bouillon
¼ teaspoon garlic powder
½ cup sour cream
2 tablespoons milk
1 (9-ounce) package refrigerated cheese filled tortellini
Warm pizza sauce or marinara sauce, for dipping

Heat oven to 400°F. In small bowl, combine bread crumbs, Parmesan cheese, bouillon and garlic powder. In another small bowl, combine sour cream and milk. Dip tortellini in sour cream mixture, then in bread crumbs; coat evenly. Place tortellini on baking sheet. Bake 10 to 12 minutes, or until crisp and golden brown; turning once. Serve immediately with warm pizza or marinara sauce.   *Makes 8 servings*

Tasty Tip: The bouillon mixture makes a great coating for chicken fingers or mild fish.

Kid Kabobs
with Cheesy Mustard Dip

Prep Time: 15 minutes

Dip

> 1 container (8 ounces) whipped cream cheese
> ¼ cup milk
> 3 tablespoons *French's®* Spicy Brown Mustard or Honey Mustard
> 2 tablespoons mayonnaise
> 2 tablespoons minced green onions

Kabobs

> ½ pound deli luncheon meat or cooked chicken and turkey, cut into 1-inch cubes
> ½ pound Swiss, Cheddar or Monterey Jack cheese, cut into 1-inch cubes
> 2 cups cut-up assorted vegetables such as broccoli, carrots, peppers, cucumbers and celery
> 16 wooden picks, about 6-inches long

1. Combine ingredients for dip in medium bowl; mix until well blended.

2. To make kabobs, place cubes of meat, cheese and chunks of vegetables on wooden picks.

3. Serve kabobs with dip.   *Makes 8 servings (about 1¼ cups dip)*

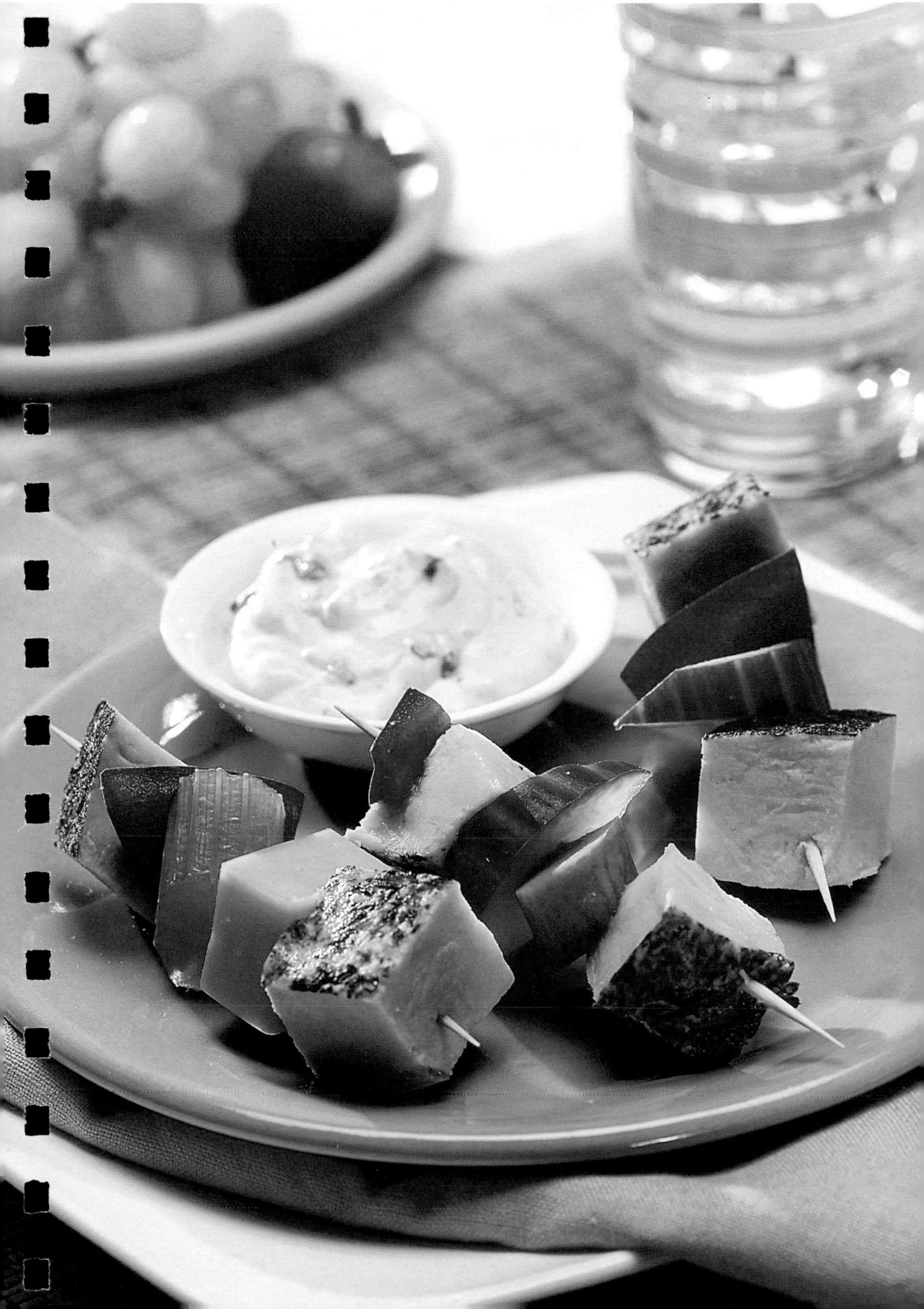

Fish
Biters

24 giant goldfish-shaped crackers
12 slices pepperoni, halved
12 Monterey Jack cheese cubes, halved
24 small black olive slices
24 flat leaf parsley leaves

1. Preheat oven to 425°F.

2. Coat large baking sheet with nonstick cooking spray.

3. Place crackers on prepared baking sheet. Place 2 pepperoni halves on tail end. Place cheese half in center of each fish. Repeat with remaining fish.

4. Bake 3 minutes or until cheese is melted. Remove from oven and immediately top with olive slice to resemble eye.

5. Lift up olive slice slightly and place a parsley leaf behind it to resemble fin. Gently press down on olive to adhere. Serve warm.

Makes 24 crackers

Tip: Fish may be assembled up to 2 hours in advance. Complete steps 1 and 2, then cover with a sheet of plastic wrap or foil and refrigerate until ready to bake.

**Mud Hole
Dunk (p. 140)**

**Snickerpoodles
(p. 130)**

Chocolate Chip Cannoli
Cones (p. 134)

Cherry Cheese Sandwich
Cookies (p. 152)

Sweet Snacks

Cracker
Toffee

72 rectangular butter-flavored crackers
1 cup (2 sticks) unsalted butter
1 cup packed brown sugar
¼ teaspoon salt
2½ cups semisweet chocolate chips
2 cups chopped pecans

1. Preheat oven to 375°F. Line 17×12-inch jelly-roll pan with heavy-duty foil. Spray generously with nonstick cooking spray. Arrange crackers with edges touching in pan; set aside.

2. Combine butter, brown sugar and salt in heavy medium saucepan. Heat over medium heat until butter melts, stirring frequently. Increase heat to high; boil 3 minutes without stirring. Pour mixture evenly over crackers; spread to cover.

3. Bake 5 minutes. Immediately sprinkle chocolate chips evenly over crackers; spread to cover. Sprinkle pecans over chocolate, pressing down. Cool to room temperature. Refrigerate 2 hours. Break into chunks to serve.
Makes 24 servings

Variation: Substitute peanut butter chips for chocolate chips and coarsely chopped, lightly salted peanuts for chopped pecans.

Snickerpoodles

1 package (18 ounces) refrigerated sugar cookie dough
1 teaspoon ground cinnamon, divided
1 teaspoon vanilla
¼ cup sugar
   Chocolate chips and mini chocolate chips
   Prepared white icing (optional)

1. Preheat oven to 350°F. Lightly grease cookie sheets. Let dough stand at room temperature about 15 minutes.

2. Combine dough, ½ teaspoon cinnamon and vanilla in large bowl; beat until well blended. Combine sugar and remaining ½ teaspoon cinnamon in small bowl. For each poodle face, shape ½ tablespoon dough into oval. Roll in cinnamon-sugar mixture; place on prepared cookie sheet. For poodle ears, divide ½ tablespoon dough in half; shape each half into teardrop shape. Roll in cinnamon-sugar mixture; place on cookie sheet at either side of face. For top of poodle head, shape scant teaspoon dough into oval. Roll in cinnamon-sugar mixture; place on cookie sheet at top of face.

3. Bake 10 to 12 minutes or until edges are lightly browned. Immediately press 1 chocolate chip and 2 mini chocolate chips upside down in face for nose and eyes. Cool 2 minutes on cookie sheets. Remove to wire racks; cool completely.

4. Decorate with icing, if desired.   *Makes about 2 dozen cookies*

Crunchy Peach
Snack Cake

1 package (9 ounces) yellow cake mix *without* pudding in the mix
1 container (6 ounces) peach yogurt
1 egg
¼ cup peach fruit spread
¾ cup square whole grain oat cereal with cinnamon, slightly crushed
Whipped cream (optional)

1. Place rack in center of oven; preheat oven to 350°F. Lightly grease 8-inch square baking pan.

2. Combine cake mix, yogurt and egg in medium bowl. Beat with electric mixer at low speed about 1 minute or until blended. Increase speed to medium; beat 1 to 2 minutes or until smooth.

3. Spread batter into prepared pan. Drop fruit spread by ½ teaspoonfuls over cake batter. Sprinkle with cereal.

4. Bake 25 minutes or until toothpick inserted into center of cake comes out clean. Cool on wire rack. Serve with whipped cream, if desired.

Makes 9 servings

Chocolate Chip
Cannoli Cones

Prep Time: 25 minutes

1¼ **cup mini chocolate chips, divided**
1 **teaspoon canola oil**
10 **sugar ice cream cones**
1 **container (15 ounces) whole milk or part-skim ricotta cheese**
⅔ **cup powdered sugar**
½ **cup thawed frozen reduced-fat whipped topping**
2 **tablespoons orange or peach marmalade**
10 **maraschino cherries**

1. Place 1 cup mini chocolate chips and oil in shallow dish and microwave 10 seconds. Stir; repeat until chips are melted. Dip edge of each cone into melted chocolate; place on waxed paper to harden or place cones in refrigerator to harden quickly, if desired.

2. Combine 2 tablespoons chocolate chips, ricotta cheese, powdered sugar, whipped topping and marmalade in medium bowl. (Mixture can be covered and refrigerated until serving time, up to 24 hours.) Spoon mixture into chocolate-dipped cones. Sprinkle 2 tablespoons remaining chocolate chips over top and place one cherry in center of each cone. Serve immediately. *Makes 10 servings*

Banana Roll-Ups

¼ cup smooth or crunchy almond butter
2 tablespoons mini chocolate chips
1 to 2 tablespoons milk
1 (8-inch) whole wheat flour tortilla
1 large banana, peeled

1. Combine almond butter, chocolate chips and 1 tablespoon milk in medium microwavable bowl. Microwave on MEDIUM (50%) 40 seconds. Stir well and repeat if necessary to melt chocolate. Add more milk if necessary for desired consistency.

2. Spread almond butter mixture on tortilla. Place banana on one side of tortilla and roll up tightly. Cut into 8 slices.   *Makes 4 servings*

Cherry S'mores

½ cup marshmallow creme
½ cup dried tart cherries
¼ cup semisweet chocolate chips
12 graham cracker squares (2½-inch squares)

Combine marshmallow creme, cherries and chocolate chips; mix well. Place 6 of the graham crackers on microwave-safe plate. Spoon heaping tablespoon of marshmallow mixture on each cracker. Top with remaining crackers.

Microwave, uncovered, on HIGH (100% Power) 30 to 45 seconds, or until marshmallow mixture is soft and warm.   *Makes 6 servings*

Note: To prepare in conventional oven, place 6 of the graham crackers in an ovenproof baking dish. Proceed as above. Bake in a preheated 350°F oven 2 to 3 minutes, or until marshmallow mixture is soft and warm.

Favorite recipe from **Cherry Marketing Institute**

Sweet
Mysteries

1 package (18¼ ounces) yellow cake mix with pudding in the mix
½ cup (1 stick) unsalted butter, softened
1 egg yolk
1 cup ground pecans
36 milk chocolate candy kisses, unwrapped
Powdered sugar

1. Preheat oven to 300°F.

2. Beat half of cake mix and butter in large bowl with electric mixer at high speed until blended. Add egg yolk and remaining cake mix; beat at medium speed just until dough forms. Add pecans; beat just until blended.

3. Shape rounded tablespoon of dough around each candy, making sure candy is completely covered. Place cookies 1 inch apart on ungreased cookie sheets.

4. Bake 20 to 25 minutes or until firm and just beginning to turn golden. Let cookies stand on cookie sheets 10 minutes. Transfer to wire racks set over waxed paper; dust with powdered sugar.   *Makes 3 dozen cookies*

Mud Hole Dunk

Prep Time: 20 minutes

4 cups fresh strawberries, cut-up fresh pineapple and seedless grapes
1 cup prepared creamy chocolate frosting*
   Assorted decorator sprinkles or flaked coconut

*Do not use whipped frosting.

1. Line baking sheet with wax paper. Set aside. Pat fruit dry with paper towels.

2. Microwave frosting on HIGH 15 to 20 seconds or until melted, stirring once.

3. Dip fruit halfway into frosting, allowing excess to drip off. Roll in desired sprinkles or coconut. Place on prepared baking sheet. Refrigerate about 10 minutes or until frosting is set.   *Makes 8 servings*

Make Ahead S'mores

8 (1-ounce) squares semisweet chocolate
1 (14-ounce) can EAGLE BRAND® Sweetened Condensed Milk (NOT evaporated milk)
1 teaspoon vanilla extract
32 (4¾×2⅛-inch) whole graham crackers
2 cups miniature marshmallows

1. In heavy saucepan, over low heat, melt chocolate with EAGLE BRAND® and vanilla; cook and stir until smooth.

2. Making 1 sandwich at a time, spread 1 tablespoon chocolate mixture on each of 2 whole graham crackers; sprinkle 1 graham cracker with marshmallows and gently press second graham cracker, chocolate side down, on top. Repeat with remaining ingredients.

3. Carefully break each sandwich in half before serving. Wrap with plastic wrap; store at room temperature.   *Makes 32 servings*

Reese's® Peanut Butter and Milk Chocolate Chip Cattails

1 cup HERSHEY'S Milk Chocolate Chips, divided
1 cup REESE'S® Peanut Butter Chips, divided
2 teaspoons shortening (do not use butter, margarine, spread or oil)
12 to 14 pretzel rods

1. Stir together milk chocolate chips and peanut butter chips. Place sheet of wax paper on tray or counter top. Finely chop 1 cup chip mixture in food processor or by hand; place on wax paper. Line tray or cookie sheet with wax paper.

2. Place remaining 1 cup chip mixture and shortening in narrow deep microwave-safe bowl. Microwave at MEDIUM (50%) 1 minute; stir. If necessary, microwave additional 30 seconds at a time, stirring after each heating, until chips are melted and mixture is smooth when stirred.

3. Spoon chocolate-peanut butter mixture over about ¾ of pretzel rod; gently shake off excess. Holding pretzel by uncoated end, roll in chopped chips, pressing chips into chocolate. Place on prepared tray. Refrigerate 30 minutes or until set. Store coated pretzels in cool, dry place.

Makes 12 to 14 coated pretzels

Variation: Melt entire package of chips with 4 teaspoons shortening and dip small pretzels into mixture.

Ooey-Gooey Pineapple Buns

Prep Time: 15 minutes • **Bake Time:** 25 minutes

⅔ cup packed brown sugar
¼ cup maple syrup
 2 tablespoons butter or margarine, melted
 1 teaspoon vanilla
 1 can (8 ounces) pineapple tidbits, drained
½ cup chopped pecans
½ cup flaked coconut
 1 package (12 ounces) refrigerated flaky biscuits
     (10 biscuits)

1. Preheat oven to 350°F. Combine brown sugar, maple syrup, butter and vanilla in 11×7×1½-inch baking pan. Sprinkle with pineapple tidbits and pecans. Sprinkle with coconut.

2. Cut biscuits into quarters. Arrange on top of coconut. Bake 25 to 30 minutes or until deep golden brown. Invert onto serving plate. Serve warm.   *Makes 10 servings*

Critter Munch

 1½ cups animal cracker cookies
 ½ (6-ounce) package Cheddar or original flavor goldfish-shaped crackers (1½ cups)
 1 cup dried tart cherries
 1 cup candy-coated chocolate candy
 1 cup honey-roasted peanuts

Put cookies, goldfish crackers, cherries, candy and peanuts in a large mixing bowl.

Carefully stir with a spoon.

Store in a tightly covered container at room temperature.

Makes 6 cups

Favorite recipe from **Cherry Marketing Institute**

Wheat and Oat Chocolate Chippers

Prep Time: 15 minutes • **Baking Time:** 9 minutes

1¼ **cups quick-cooking rolled oats**
¼ **cup plus 2 tablespoons all-purpose flour**
¼ **cup plus 2 tablespoons whole wheat flour**
½ **teaspoon baking soda**
¼ **cup plus 2 tablespoons granulated sugar**
¼ **cup plus 2 tablespoons packed brown sugar**
¼ **cup (½ stick) butter or margarine, softened**
¼ **cup shortening**
1 **egg**
½ **teaspoon vanilla**
½ **cup mini semisweet chocolate chips**
½ **cup dried cranberries**

1. Preheat oven to 375°F. Combine oats, flours and baking soda in large bowl. Set aside.

2. Beat granulated sugar, brown sugar, butter and shortening in large bowl with electric mixer at medium-high speed until combined. Add egg and vanilla; beat until light and fluffy. Add oat mixture. Beat at low speed until combined. Stir in chocolate chips and cranberries.

3. Drop by rounded teaspoonfuls onto ungreased baking sheets. Bake 9 to 11 minutes or until lightly browned. Remove to wire racks; cool completely. *Makes 2½ dozen cookies*

Secret Ingredient Brownies

Prep Time: 15 minutes • **Bake Time:** 30 minutes

1 cup packed brown sugar
1 cup applesauce
½ cup (1 stick) butter or margarine, melted
2 eggs
1 teaspoon vanilla
1 cup all-purpose flour
⅓ cup unsweetened cocoa powder
⅓ cup mini chocolate chips
2 teaspoons baking powder
2 teaspoons baking soda
½ teaspoon salt
½ teaspoon ground cinnamon
⅓ cup powdered sugar

1. Preheat oven to 350°F. Spray 8-inch square pan with nonstick cooking spray. Whisk together brown sugar, applesauce, butter, eggs and vanilla in large bowl until well blended. Stir in flour, cocoa powder, chocolate chips, baking powder, baking soda, salt and cinnamon; mix well.

2. Pour batter into prepared pan. Bake 30 to 35 minutes or until edges begin to pull away from sides of pan and toothpick inserted into center comes out clean. Cool in pan on wire rack. Dust with powdered sugar just before serving. Cut into squares to serve.   *Makes 16 brownies*

Note: Brownies will stay fresh up to 3 days. Simply wrap and store and room temperature.

S'mores with an Oatmeal Twist

8 large oatmeal cookies
½ thin chocolate candy bar, broken into squares
8 slices banana
4 marshmallows

1. Place one cookie flat side up on serving plate. Top with 2 chocolate squares and 2 banana slices.

2. Toast marshmallows;* place one marshmallow on top of each pair of banana slices. Top with another cookie, flat side down. Serve immediately.

Makes 4 servings

*To toast marshmallows, place on a wooden skewer and hold over low flame of gas stove, rotating to toast all sides.

Polar Bear Banana Bites

1 medium banana, cut into 6 equal-size pieces
¼ cup creamy peanut butter*
3 tablespoons fat-free (skim) milk
¼ cup mini marshmallows
2 tablespoons unsalted dry-roasted peanuts, chopped (optional)
1 tablespoon chocolate-flavored decorator sprinkles

*Soy butter or almond butter can be used in place of peanut butter.

1. Insert toothpick into each banana piece. Place on wax paper-lined tray.

2. Whisk together peanut butter and milk. Combine marshmallows, peanuts, if desired, and chocolate sprinkles in shallow dish. Dip each banana piece in peanut butter mixture, draining off excess. Roll in marshmallow mixture. Place on tray; let stand until set.

Makes 3 servings

Ooey-Gooey Caramel Peanut Butter Bars

1 package (18¼ ounces) yellow cake mix *without* pudding in the mix
1 cup uncooked quick-cooking oats
⅔ cup creamy peanut butter
1 egg, slightly beaten
2 tablespoons milk
1 package (8 ounces) cream cheese, softened
1 jar (12¼ ounces) caramel ice cream topping
1 cup semisweet chocolate chips

1. Preheat oven to 350°F. Lightly grease 13×9-inch baking pan.

2. Combine cake mix and oats in large bowl. Cut in peanut butter with pastry blender or 2 knives until mixture is crumbly.

3. Blend egg and milk in small bowl. Add to peanut butter mixture; stir just until combined. Reserve 1½ cups mixture. Press remaining peanut butter mixture into prepared pan.

4. Beat cream cheese in small bowl with electric mixer on medium speed until fluffy. Add caramel topping; beat just until combined. Carefully spread over peanut butter layer in pan. Break up reserved peanut butter mixture into small pieces; sprinkle over cream cheese layer. Sprinkle with chocolate chips.

5. Bake about 30 minutes or until nearly set in center. Cool completely in pan on wire rack. *Makes 24 bars*

Cherry Cheese Sandwich Cookies

1 package (8 ounces) reduced-fat cream cheese, softened
¼ cup powdered sugar, sifted
¼ cup cherry preserves
2 tablespoons chopped dried cherries
¼ teaspoon vanilla or almond extract
40 vanilla cookies

1. Beat cream cheese in medium bowl with electric mixer at medium speed. Mix in sugar, preserves, cherries and vanilla until well blended; refrigerate 30 minutes.

2. Spoon about 2 teaspoons cream cheese mixture onto flat side of one cookie. Top with another cookie, flat side down. Repeat with remaining cookies and filling. Serve immediately. *Makes 10 servings*

Tip: Try strawberry, raspberry or other preserve flavors to suit your child's tastes.

Monkey Parfaits

Prep Time: 10 minutes

1 banana, sliced
1 container (8 ounces) strawberry yogurt
1 cup seedless red grapes or pitted cherries, halved
½ cup flaked coconut (optional)
½ cup mandarin oranges, drained
4 grapes or pitted cherries

1. Layer one-fourth of banana, yogurt, grapes, coconut, if desired, and oranges in each of 4 parfait glasses.

2. Top each serving with one whole grape. *Makes 4 servings*

Stuffed
Banana Smiles

Prep Time: 2 minutes • **Bake Time:** 1 minute

1 medium size banana, with peel on
1 tablespoon SUN-MAID® Raisins or Golden Raisins
1 tablespoon semi-sweet, milk or white chocolate baking chips

1. **PLACE** banana, with peel on, flat on its side on a microwave-safe plate.

2. **STARTING*** and ending ¼-inch from the ends of banana, cut a slit lengthwise through the banana up to the skin on the other side.

3. **GENTLY** open the banana. Use your fingers to stuff the banana with raisins, then add chocolate chips.

4. **MICROWAVE*** banana uncovered on HIGH for 40 to 60 seconds or until chocolate begins to melt and banana is still firm. Banana skin may darken slightly. Eat immediately, scooping with a spoon right out of the banana peel.   *Makes 1 serving*

Tip: At a party, invite guests to prepare their own banana smile!

Tip: To prepare on grill,* place each banana flat on its side on a piece of aluminum foil and follow steps 2 and 3 above. Wrap bananas loosely and pinch foil closed. Place on covered grill or over hot coals for about 5 minutes or just until chocolate begins to melt and banana is still firm.

Tip: To prepare in oven,* place each banana flat on its side on a piece of aluminum foil and follow steps 2 and 3 above. Wrap bananas loosely and pinch foil closed. Place on a baking sheet and bake in the oven at 350°F for 5 minutes.

*Adult Supervision Suggested

The publisher would like to thank the companies and organizations listed below for the use of their recipes and photographs in this publication.

Cherry Marketing Institute

Dole Food Company, Inc.

EAGLE BRAND®

The Hershey Company

Hormel Foods, LLC

© Mars, Incorporated 2007

National Watermelon Promotion Board

Reckitt Benckiser Inc.

Sun•Maid® Growers of California

Unilever

Wheat Foods Council

A
Apple and Cheese Pockets, 46
Apples
Apple and Cheese Pockets, 46
Bedrock Fruit Boulders, 84
Happy Apple Salsa with Baked
   Cinnamon Pita Chips, 22
Peanut Butter-Apple Wraps, 30
Warm Peanut-Caramel Dip, 20

B
Baby Bran Muffins with Citrus Spread,
   18
Bacon
BLT Cukes, 14
Turkey Bacon Mini Wafflewiches, 54
Baked Taco Chicken Bites, 90
Banana Caterpillars, 6
Banana Roll-Ups, 136
Banana Tot Pops, 32
Bananas
Banana Caterpillars, 6
Banana Roll-Ups, 136
Banana Tot Pops, 32
Fun Fruit Kabobs, 82
Jiggly Banana Split, 26
Jungle Juice, 116
Monkey Parfaits, 152
Polar Bear Banana Bites, 148
Pretty Pink Pies, 74
S'mores with an Oatmeal Twist, 148
Stuffed Banana Smiles, 154
Bear Bite Snack Mix, 82
Bedrock Fruit Boulders, 84
Beef
Earth's Core Meatballs, 38
Sammich Swirls, 62
Beverages
Chillin' Out Watermelon Soda, 28
Jungle Juice, 116
BLT Cukes, 14
Breakfast Mice, 24
Brownies and Bars
Ooey-Gooey Caramel Peanut Butter
   Bars, 150
Secret Ingredient Brownies, 174

C
Cakes & Cupcakes
Cookie Pizza Cake, 94
Crunchy Peach Snack Cake, 132
Doodle Bug Cupcakes, 88

Cakes & Cupcakes (continued)
Double Chocolate Chip Snack Cake,
   70
Gooey Coconut Chocolate
   Cupcakes, 100
Meteorite Mini Cakes, 74
Candy Corn by the Slice, 54
Caramel Popcorn Balls, 118
Cheddar Broccoli Martians, 92
Cheesy Snails, 106
Cherry
Cherry Cheese Sandwich Cookies,
   152
Cherry S'mores, 136
Critter Munch, 144
Cherry Cheese Sandwich Cookies, 152
Cherry S'mores, 136
Cherry Tomato Planets, 90
Cherry Tomato Pops, 110
Chicken
Baked Taco Chicken Bites, 90
Frogs & Ladybugs, 58
Mucho Gusto Pizza, 48
You Make Me Dizzy Sub, 96
Chillin' Out Watermelon Soda, 28
Chocolate
Double Chocolate Chip Snack Cake,
   70
Mud Hole Dunk, 140
Pretzel Fried Eggs, 108
Secret Ingredient Brownies, 174
Chocolate (see also **Chocolate
   Chips**)
Chocolate Panini Bites, 112
Clown-Around Cones, 86
Cookie Pizza Cake, 94
Critter Munch, 144
Give Me S'more Muffins, 114
Gooey Coconut Chocolate
   Cupcakes, 100
Make Ahead S'mores, 140
"M&M's"® Family Party Mix, 80
Meteorite Mini Cakes, 74
S'mores with an Oatmeal Twist, 148
Sweet Mysteries, 138
Chocolate Chip Cannoli Cones, 134
Chocolate Chips
Caramel Popcorn Balls, 118
Chocolate Chip Cannoli Cones, 134
Cracker Toffee, 128
Double Chocolate Chip Snack Cake,
   70

Chocolate Chips *(continued)*
Give Me S'more Muffins, 114
Ooey-Gooey Caramel Peanut Butter Bars, 150
Popcorn Truffles, 104
Reese's® Peanut Butter and Milk Chocolate Chip Cattails, 142
S'mores on a Stick, 76
Wheat and Oat Chocolate Chippers, 146
Chocolate Panini Bites, 112
Chunky Chews, 112
Cinnamon Toast Poppers, 120
Clown-Around Cones, 86
Coconut
Caramel Popcorn Balls, 118
Gooey Coconut Chocolate Cupcakes, 100
Ooey-Gooey Pineapple Buns, 144
Cookie Pizza Cake, 94
Cookies
Cherry Cheese Sandwich Cookies, 152
Snickerpoodles, 130
Sweet Mysteries, 138
Wheat and Oat Chocolate Chippers, 146
Corny Face, 56
Cracker Toffee, 128
Crescent Moons, 62
Crisp Tortellini Bites, 120
Critter Munch, 144
Crunchy Peach Snack Cake, 132

D
Dips
Funny Face Cheese Ball, 72
Happy Apple Salsa with Baked Cinnamon Pita Chips, 22
Kid Kabobs with Cheesy Mustard Dip, 122
Peaches and Creamy Dip with Waffle Wedges, 28
Warm Peanut-Caramel Dip, 20
Watermelon Dippers, 32
Doodle Bug Cupcakes, 88
Double Chocolate Chip Snack Cake, 70

E
Earth's Core Meatballs, 38

F
Fish: Melting Tuna Calzone, 47
Fish Biters, 124
Focaccia Bars, 50
Frogs & Ladybugs, 58
Frozen Snacks
Banana Tot Pops, 32
Clown-Around Cones, 86
Orange You Glad Dessert, 16
Peachy Pops, 10
Fun Fruit Kabobs, 82
Funny Face Cheese Ball, 72
Funny Face Pizza Snacks, 8

G
Give Me S'more Muffins, 114
Gooey Coconut Chocolate Cupcakes, 100
Granola Sunshine, 110

H
Ham
Crescent Moons, 62
Ham and Potato Pancakes, 40
Inside-Out Breadsticks, 64
Luscious Veggie Sandwich Spread, 30
Peanutty Ham Turnovers, 66
Pizza Fondue, 98
Tic-Tac-Toe Sandwich, 52
Waffled Grilled Cheese, 48
You Make Me Dizzy Sub, 96
Ham and Potato Pancakes, 40
Happy Apple Salsa with Baked Cinnamon Pita Chips, 22

I
Inside-Out Breadsticks, 64

J
Jiggly Banana Split, 26
Jungle Juice, 116

K
Kid Kabobs with Cheesy Mustard Dip, 122

L
Luau Fruit Cups, 34
Luscious Veggie Sandwich Spread, 30

M
Make Ahead S'mores, 140
"M&M's"® Family Party Mix, 80
Marshmallows
  Cherry S'mores, 136
  Give Me S'more Muffins, 114
  Granola Sunshine, 110
  Make Ahead S'mores, 140
  S'mores on a Stick, 76
  S'mores with an Oatmeal Twist, 148
Melting Tuna Calzone, 47
Meteorite Mini Cakes, 74
Mini Cheese Burritos, 60
Monkey Parfaits, 152
Mucho Gusto Pizza, 48
Mud Hole Dunk, 140
Muffins
  Baby Bran Muffins with Citrus
    Spread, 18
  Give Me S'more Muffins, 114
Mysterious Colorful Jiggles, 78

N
Nuts
  Cracker Toffee, 128
  Critter Munch, 144
  "M&M's"® Family Party Mix, 80
  Ooey-Gooey Pineapple Buns, 144
  Peanutty Ham Turnovers, 66
  Sweet Mysteries, 138

O
Ooey-Gooey Caramel Peanut Butter
  Bars, 150
Ooey-Gooey Pineapple Buns, 144
Orange
  Monkey Parfaits, 152
  Orange You Glad Dessert, 16
Orange You Glad Dessert, 16

P
Peach
  Crunchy Peach Snack Cake, 132
  Peaches and Creamy Dip with Waffle
    Wedges, 28
  Peachy Pops, 10
Peaches and Creamy Dip with Waffle
  Wedges, 28
Peachy Pops, 10
Peanut Butter
  Chunky Chews, 112
  Cookie Pizza Cake, 94

Peanut Butter (continued)
  Ooey-Gooey Caramel Peanut Butter
    Bars, 150
  Peanut Butter-Apple Wraps, 30
  Reese's® Peanut Butter and Milk
    Chocolate Chip Cattails, 142
  Warm Peanut-Caramel Dip, 20
Peanut Butter-Apple Wraps, 30
Peanutty Ham Turnovers, 66
Pies: Pretty Pink Pies, 74
Pineapple
  Luau Fruit Cups, 34
  Mud Hole Dunk, 140
  Ooey-Gooey Pineapple Buns, 144
Pizza
  Candy Corn by the Slice, 54
  Cookie Pizza Cake, 94
  Focaccia Bars, 50
  Funny Face Pizza Snacks, 8
  Mucho Gusto Pizza, 48
  Pizza Dippin' Strips, 80
  Pizza Fondue, 98
  Veggie Pizza Pitas, 101
Pizza Dippin' Strips, 80
Pizza Fondue, 98
Polar Bear Banana Bites, 148
Popcorn
  Caramel Popcorn Balls, 118
  Popcorn Truffles, 104
Popcorn Truffles, 104
Potatoes
  Ham and Potato Pancakes, 40
  Sweet Potato Spread Sandwich, 12
Pretty Pink Pies, 74
Pretzel Fried Eggs, 108

R
Raisins
  Bear Bite Snack Mix, 82
  "M&M's"® Family Party Mix, 80
Reese's® Peanut Butter and Milk
  Chocolate Chip Cattails, 142

S
S'mores on a Stick, 76
S'mores with an Oatmeal Twist, 148
Sammich Swirls, 62
Sandwiches
  Chocolate Panini Bites, 112
  Luscious Veggie Sandwich Spread,
    30
  Peanut Butter-Apple Wraps, 30

Sandwiches *(continued)*
Sammich Swirls, 62
Sloppy Joe Race Cars, 42
Spotted Butterfly Sandwich, 44
Sweet Potato Spread Sandwich, 12
Tic-Tac-Toe Sandwich, 52
Turkey Bacon Mini Wafflewiches, 54
Waffled Grilled Cheese, 48
You Make Me Dizzy Sub, 96
Sausage
Cherry Tomato Planets, 90
Fish Biters, 124
Pizza Dippin' Strips, 80
Pizza Fondue, 98
You Make Me Dizzy Sub, 96
Secret Ingredient Brownies, 174
Sloppy Joe Race Cars, 42
Snickerpoodles, 130
Spotted Butterfly Sandwich, 44
Strawberry
Fun Fruit Kabobs, 82
Jungle Juice, 116
Luau Fruit Cups, 34
Monkey Parfaits, 152
Mud Hole Dunk, 140
Pretty Pink Pies, 74
Stuffed Banana Smiles, 154
Sweet Mysteries, 138
Sweet Potato Spread Sandwich, 12

T
Tic-Tac-Toe Sandwich, 52
Ticos Fricos, 104
Turkey
Sloppy Joe Race Cars, 42
Turkey Bacon Mini Wafflewiches, 54
Turkey Tacos, 52
Watermelon Kebobs, 8
Turkey Bacon Mini Wafflewiches, 54
Turkey Tacos, 52
Twisted Dunkers, 116

V
Vegetables
BLT Cukes, 14
Cheddar Broccoli Martians, 92
Cherry Tomato Pops, 110
Earth's Core Meatballs, 38
Funny-Face Cheese Ball, 72
Kid Kabobs with Cheesy Mustard Dip, 122

Vegetables *(continued)*
Luscious Veggie Sandwich Spread, 30
Melting Tuna Calzones, 46
Turkey Tacos, 52
Veggie Pizza Pitas, 101
Zucchini Circles, 17
Veggie Pizza Pitas, 101

W
Waffled Grilled Cheese, 48
Warm Peanut-Caramel Dip, 20
Watermelon
Chillin' Out Watermelon Soda, 28
Watermelon Dippers, 32
Watermelon Kebobs, 8
Watermelon Dippers, 32
Watermelon Kebobs, 8
Wheat and Oat Chocolate Chippers, 146
White Chocolate
Double Chocolate Chip Snack Cake, 70
Pretzel Fried Eggs, 108

Y
You Make Me Dizzy Sub, 96

Z
Zucchini Circles, 17

VOLUME MEASUREMENTS (dry)

1/8 teaspoon = 0.5 mL
1/4 teaspoon = 1 mL
1/2 teaspoon = 2 mL
3/4 teaspoon = 4 mL
1 teaspoon = 5 mL
1 tablespoon = 15 mL
2 tablespoons = 30 mL
1/4 cup = 60 mL
1/3 cup = 75 mL
1/2 cup = 125 mL
2/3 cup = 150 mL
3/4 cup = 175 mL
1 cup = 250 mL
2 cups = 1 pint = 500 mL
3 cups = 750 mL
4 cups = 1 quart = 1 L

VOLUME MEASUREMENTS (fluid)

1 fluid ounce (2 tablespoons) = 30 mL
4 fluid ounces (1/2 cup) = 125 mL
8 fluid ounces (1 cup) = 250 mL
12 fluid ounces (1 1/2 cups) = 375 mL
16 fluid ounces (2 cups) = 500 mL

WEIGHTS (mass)

1/2 ounce = 15 g
1 ounce = 30 g
3 ounces = 90 g
4 ounces = 120 g
8 ounces = 225 g
10 ounces = 285 g
12 ounces = 360 g
16 ounces = 1 pound = 450 g

DIMENSIONS

1/16 inch = 2 mm
1/8 inch = 3 mm
1/4 inch = 6 mm
1/2 inch = 1.5 cm
3/4 inch = 2 cm
1 inch = 2.5 cm

OVEN TEMPERATURES

250°F = 120°C
275°F = 140°C
300°F = 150°C
325°F = 160°C
350°F = 180°C
375°F = 190°C
400°F = 200°C
425°F = 220°C
450°F = 230°C

BAKING PAN SIZES

Utensil	Size in Inches/Quarts	Metric Volume	Size in Centimeters
Baking or Cake Pan (square or rectangular)	8 × 8 × 2	2 L	20 × 20 × 5
	9 × 9 × 2	2.5 L	23 × 23 × 5
	12 × 8 × 2	3 L	30 × 20 × 5
	13 × 9 × 2	3.5 L	33 × 23 × 5
Loaf Pan	8 × 4 × 3	1.5 L	20 × 10 × 7
	9 × 5 × 3	2 L	23 × 13 × 7
Round Layer Cake Pan	8 × 1½	1.2 L	20 × 4
	9 × 1½	1.5 L	23 × 4
Pie Plate	8 × 1¼	750 mL	20 × 3
	9 × 1¼	1 L	23 × 3
Baking Dish or Casserole	1 quart	1 L	—
	1½ quart	1.5 L	—
	2 quart	2 L	—